David Skinner is a Baptist minist_ East Reading for over 17 years, h_ background in community-based ministry exploring innovative ways to work with schools and students to tap into their innate interest in spiritual issues. David has co-authored Spiritual Engagement, *a thought-provoking resource for churches and teachers, to inspire all 16 to 19-year-olds through RE day conferences.*

Paul Haynes is project director of REinspired. Before joining REinspired in 2008, he worked as a project manager in the IT industry for over 20 years. Paul became a Christian in 1990 and since then he has been involved in various local church ministries, working with children and young people in churches and the local community. Paul's vision is to see the REinspired model of working with schools taken up across the country.

Jane Earl has been chair of the trustees of REinspired for the past three years. She is a former senior civil servant, and was chief executive of a local council. She has three children, all of whom have had their lives touched by the work of REinspired in their school careers. She is a member of her local Methodist Church.

Barnabas for Children ® is a registered word mark and the logo is a registered device mark of The Bible Reading Fellowship.

Text copyright © David Skinner, Paul Haynes and Jane Earl 2011
The authors assert the moral right
to be identified as the authors of this work

Published by
The Bible Reading Fellowship
15 The Chambers, Vineyard
Abingdon OX14 3FE
United Kingdom
Tel: +44 (0)1865 319700
Email: enquiries@brf.org.uk
Website: www.brf.org.uk
BRF is a Registered Charity

ISBN 978 1 84101 771 6
First published 2010
10 9 8 7 6 5 4 3 2 1 0
All rights reserved

Acknowledgments
Unless otherwise stated, scripture quotations are taken from the Contemporary English Version of the Bible published by HarperCollins Publishers, copyright © 1991, 1992, 1995 American Bible Society.

Scripture quotations taken from the Holy Bible, New International Version, copyright © 1973, 1978, 1984 by International Bible Society, are used by permission of Hodder & Stoughton Publishers, a member of the Hachette Livre UK Group. All rights reserved. 'NIV' is a registered trademark of International Bible Society. UK trademark number 1448790.

Scriptures quoted from the Good News Bible published by The Bible Societies/HarperCollins Publishers Ltd, UK © American Bible Society 1966, 1971, 1976, 1992, used with permission.

A catalogue record for this book is available from the British Library

Printed in Singapore by Craft Print International Ltd

The Story of REinspired

Developing creative partnerships between churches and schools

David Skinner, Paul Haynes and Jane Earl

For the teachers and students of the Earley and East Reading Schools who have patiently taught us so much, and for all the volunteers and staff of REinspired who have made this vision come alive.

Acknowledgments

We are indebted to many for their help in the writing of this book. In particular we would like to thank the staff at BRF, especially our editor Sue Doggett for her thoughtful help, and Richard Fisher and Karen Laister for encouraging us in this endeavour.

We also want to acknowledge the contribution of everyone who has partnered with us and helped to shape REinspired.

The head teachers, RE coordinators, class teachers and pupils in Aldryngton, Alfred Sutton, Earley St Peter's, Hillside, Hawkedon, St John's, Loddon, Newtown, Radstock, Redlands and Whiteknights primary schools and Maiden Erlegh and Bulmershe secondary schools. We thank them for welcoming us, for their enthusiasm, for their patience and for their honest feedback.

Alfie Hay and Helen Currie, RE Advisers for the Reading and Wokingham local authorities, for all their help and advice.

Jo Fageant, RE Adviser of the Oxford Diocese, Canon David Winter, Lat Blaylock of *RE Today*, Chris Curtis of the Luton Churches Education Trust, who as wise counsellors have inspired, supported and guided our journey.

To the trusts that have made grants to REinspired, especially: Baptist Union of Great Britain, Jerusalem Trust, Reading St Laurence Lands Trust, Kiriath Trust, Edgar Millward Charity, Englefield Charitable Trust, Sarum St Michael Educational Charity and the Culham Educational Foundation.

To all the churches in Churches Together in Earley and East Reading and other local churches and their members who actively, prayerfully and financially support us.

Those who have served as trustees: Elaine Watts, Dan Tyndall,

Rob Weston, Bob Harland, Gordon Guile, Keith Wilson and Honor Alleyne. Emma West, for all her expertise as our treasurer; Margaret Barnes and Patricia Brown for their tireless work. Our advocates in local churches who promote REinspired among their congregations. Our other advisers, Katie Aldridge, Catherine Edwards, Alan Harland and Cecile Gillard and her team at Jordans Limited.

Our former Project Managers, Simon Howard and Pete Stone, who laid down such good foundations for us to build on, and Wendy Neale whose administrative gifts have been invaluable.

Our fantastic primary team leaders, Alison Chevassut, Julia Jones, Sue Rees and Suzanne Knight, whose fresh ideas, creativity and diligence underpin the vitality of what REinspired does. Linda Galpin, who now heads up REinspired in Woodley. Thanks for your encouragement and your enthusiastic storytelling.

Finally, we thank all our volunteers and helpers. Space precludes naming you but your sharing of your faith, time and talents is the most important contribution of all.

REinspired seeks...

- To be a resource for schools in the achievement of their educational goals.
- To foster their growth as institutions that support and encourage the spiritual development of all their members.
- To enable pupils to develop spiritually in collective worship and other contexts.
- To create opportunities for pupils to understand and perceive the relevance of Christian spirituality in today's world and discover what they can learn from it.
- To provide positive opportunities in Religious Education (RE) for pupils to learn about and learn from Christianity.
- To offer pastoral support and care to school communities.
- To help churches, schools and pupils to value and respect people of different faiths alongside Christianity.

Endorsements

With their thorough understanding of the curriculum and education system, and their professional and prayerful interactions with churches and schools, the REinspired team model the best practice for Christian schools work today. If you are willing to learn about 'how to do Christian schools work', then start with this book!
Alison Farnell, Christian education writer, trainer and consultant; former Director of The Stapleford Centre

It's hard to think of anything in the field of Christian mission, in its broadest sense, more strategic than encouraging schools to think seriously about faith issues. That was and is the vision of Reinspired, which began in Reading but serves as a model for similar projects in other parts of the UK. It requires, as this book makes clear, dedication, tact, sensitivity and skill—but the end product is an open door into young people's understanding of life. All I can say is, I've seen it, and it works.
Canon David Winter, author and broadcaster

Pioneering initiatives are mostly out of reach for ordinary churches. REinspired is a welcome exception. This excellent overview tells their story alongside demonstrating the principles and working practice that have proven so successful. Local churches, working together, really can support the educational objectives of the schools in their community as they share their experience as people of faith.
Dr Roger Standing, Director of Training, Spurgeon's College

REinspired is a living, breathing expression of Christian unity. At its heart is excellent RE and a clear understanding of the difference between evangelisation and education. My hope and prayer is that many churches will catch this vision, engage with their local schools and offer a dynamic encounter with living Christian faith.
Sarah Lane Cawte, Education Officer, Churches Together in England and the Free Churches' Group

Contents

Foreword 9

Introduction 10

Part One: Getting it

1. From small beginnings 18
2. Discovering that difference is great 24
3. Respect 30
4. 'E' is for education 36
5. Aiming high and building strong 42
6. Partnership 49
7. Hot tips! 54

Part Two: Doing something with it

8. Creating a session (1) 62
9. Creating a session (2) 67
10. Nuts and bolts 71
11. Spots, journalists and the arts 78
12. Difficult issues and challenging choices 88
13. The creation and evolution of REinspired 94
14. It's a gift 98
15. A bigger project and an exciting question 101

16 Mission that will change your church 106

Epilogue 108

Appendices

Appendix One: Lesson plans.. 112

Spots began to appear on the earth (Reception)

The parable of the lost sheep (Years 1 and 2)

A church visit (Key Stage One)

Faith and the arts (Key Stage Two)

Death, funerals and the Christian response (Years 5 and 6)

Appendix Two: Sample risk assessment 138

Appendix Three: Templates 143

Death, funerals and the Christian response worksheet

Dragonfly craft activity

Waterbugs and dragonflies sheet

Dragonfly wings and body

Foreword

My parents have a painting in their house entitled *The Call of Samuel*. It depicts a young boy standing by the side of an old man. It seems to be night. The old man is listening carefully while the boy tries to convey something of great importance. But what is it? Who are these people? And what is happening in the picture? If you know a bit about the Bible, you'll know the answers to these questions straightaway. But if you don't, you are cut off from so much of the culture that has shaped the art and literature of our nation.

The story behind the picture is found in 1 Samuel 3. It is about the young boy Samuel hearing a voice calling him in the night. He thinks it is the priest, Eli, but Eli sends him back to bed. When Samuel hears the voice a third time, Eli realises it is God speaking and tells Samuel to respond by saying, 'I'm listening.' Thus Samuel's own understanding of God's purpose for his life begins.

We all have a sense of God's presence. Therefore, education must include exploration of this aspect of our common humanity. Not just so we can understand our culture (although without it a lot will be difficult to understand) but because faith is a living tradition that shapes people's lives today, and a vitally important force in the world.

Schools are required to teach RE and most of them are only too pleased to have some help when it is offered in an appropriate and professional way. They want the sort of partnership that REinspired has offered so brilliantly in Reading. Indeed, as Bishop of Reading from 2004 to 2010, I had the privilege of seeing some of their work at first hand. The story of REinspired is simply the story of people from different churches getting together and serving their local schools to make RE come alive. This brings us back to the painting. In listening, Samuel found that God had a purpose for his life. The story of REinspired is about listening, and joining in with God's purposes.

The Right Revd Stephen Cottrell, Bishop of Chelmsford

*

Introduction

'It's not rocket science!' explained one of our greatest supporters. 'Many people don't get it when they first hear about it, but when they do, it's so easy to understand.' We're writing this book hoping that all sorts of people may 'get it' and be encouraged to do something 'with it'. We're not trying to tell you everything you must do but to share with you some simple insights which, we've discovered, unleash enormous creativity. For us, they have been key principles in building a more confident relationship between local schools and local churches.

You might be a Christian parent whose child attends the local primary school, looking with other like-minded parents for ways to offer some support to hard-pressed staff. Perhaps you're a teacher in that school, uncertain how to engage local churches to support your teaching of Christianity in RE. You might attend the local church and be passionate that the faith you love should be better understood by the rising generation, when it is so often poorly presented in the media that influence them. You might be a church leader who's aware of the need, or even believes you are being challenged by God, to develop a relationship with a local school. Whoever you are, we hope that this book will inspire you to explore with others just how much can be so easily achieved.

Our story arises out of a moment of spiritual inspiration. One of our local schools had taken a decision not to invite in any outside speakers from faith communities. Such visits had seemed 'too difficult' to attempt. However, under pressure from school inspectors, an approach was made to a local church to see if some input could be offered to the teaching of RE.

A meeting followed between two probationary teachers and a local minister. The school was initially uncertain how we might help. However, it was open to receiving two visits in the autumn term, which was when the block of teaching about Christianity took place for their classes. In search of a good place to begin, the locally agreed RE syllabus was pulled out and it was decided that we would look for ways to support the teaching on the first three subject areas: 'Why do Christians think Jesus is special?', 'Jesus' baptism' and 'The story of Jesus' temptation in the desert'. In addition, we agreed to lead a session about Christmas.

The inspirational thought occurred that it would be far more creative for pupils to visit local churches than for a church leader to go into the school. There would be an exciting learning opportunity for Year 4 if they were to explore their RE teaching on Christianity in the atmosphere of a building used for Christian worship. It would be a large and flexible space, filled with the artefacts they were studying and alongside people who knew that faith on the inside. The possibility of pupils being engaged by a team of Christians rather than a single church leader would be far more interesting. Also, to ease the school's fears that such visits might result in inappropriate attempts to lead students into confessional Christianity, it was suggested that the team delivering the sessions should be ecumenical.

The promise was made at the end of July, in faith that it would be possible to create a team and prepare the first session for the beginning of the next term. It was a frantic summer, trying to identify the gifted and simply the willing from across five local churches. Then a session had to be developed which covered these three big subject areas, which would be interesting to the students, useful to the school and last no more than 75 minutes. The team consisted of people from the Community and Catholic churches as well as Anglican, United Reformed and Baptist churches. There were about ten of us, including two ministers and a children's worker.

The children arrived, excited to be out of school and in a new and interesting place. The session started with a child's question. His hand had been up from the moment he sat down. 'Sir, Sir, why have you got a swimming pool in your church?' We were in a Baptist church and the session was going to include not only a projection of pictures of where Jesus might have been baptised in the River Jordan but an even more visual demonstration of believer's baptism. The baptistry was full of water and the need to ask was overwhelming. When we reached that part of the session, every pupil's attention was completely focused and you could have heard a pin drop. It was a delight to see 60 young people learning about 'living faith', engaged, enjoying and captivated by their study, all of which was taking place in a church building. It was far from perfect, but the teachers liked it as well.

Over the next few years, the school increasingly negotiated more sessions so that, after four years, every pupil in every year was visiting a local church at least once to share in a dynamic, interactive and, above all, fun RE session. It was then that other schools began to make similar requests for support with their RE. It would have been extremely worthwhile even if our engagement with that first school had been the only ongoing result. However, ten years on we are delivering nearly 100 primary sessions to around 4600 primary students drawn from all of our eleven local primary schools each year. Usually, a whole year group from a school will visit a local church to receive an RE session which supports the teaching of Christianity in their school syllabus.

So what is it that attracts schools and their local churches to work alongside each other?

At its heart, it is about being inspired and making Christianity come alive in RE. It is about enabling Christians to share their faith openly with pupils. It is definitely not about avoiding either the difficult or the spiritual, but it is about handling those elements well and handling them together with the teaching staff. It is always about working with the staff to help the students reach their learning goals, and it must be enjoyable, fascinating, challenging and irresistible for the pupils as well as the teachers and volunteers. There are rarely any moments when pupils misbehave or lose

Introduction

concentration. If there are, it's usually because we ourselves are not concentrating.

Here's what some teachers and educationalists have said about what we do.

The group has been most inspired and, over the years, has invented wonderful work to involve our children. The pilgrimage day was fantastic —the children really enjoyed that.

JULIE HATHERLY, PRIMARY TEACHER, NEW TOWN PRIMARY SCHOOL

Children and staff were warmly welcomed and encouraged to participate throughout. The children learnt about Advent and the real meaning of Christmas. Their vocabulary was extended while watching exciting and colourful presentations and talks.

YEAR 1 TEACHERS AT WHITEKNIGHTS PRIMARY SCHOOL

It's great that REinspired now come into school and run their workshops here. They are always well organised, with the resources needed readily available for the children to use. A good variety of teaching approaches and activities are used.

DEBBIE BELL, TEACHER AT RADSTOCK PRIMARY SCHOOL

REinspired visits enable children to meet and hear people of faith talking about their faith. Faith moves from the abstract to the real. It is so important, when children are learning about religion, that they meet believers, and this is what is so great about REinspired. The interactive nature of the sessions helps promote a positive picture of faith and of the subject.

MARGARET ELCOCK, PRIMARY TEACHER, RE COORDINATOR AND SACRE MEMBER

At St Peter's School we greatly value our close links with REinspired. As a Church of England school we aim to provide our pupils with a varied and exciting Religious Education curriculum. We believe we do this within school. However, by working with REinspired we are able to

offer the children far more than would otherwise be possible.

The children greatly look forward to their REinspired sessions, which are always well planned, presented and resourced and add to the children's perception that RE is an exciting subject. From a teachers' perspective, the sessions provide a high level of expert input.

Both our last OFSTED report and our last Church School Inspection report talk about the outstanding spiritual and moral development of St Peter's pupils. I believe that REinspired and, more particularly, every individual who represents it and works for it can quite rightly say that, through their work with our children, they have played a vital role in, and have been part of, the school achieving those standards.

STEVE SCOTT, HEAD TEACHER AT EARLEY ST PETER'S PRIMARY SCHOOL

REinspired does exactly what it says on the tin. In our schools it has given encouragement to our teachers to explore issues of faith and culture by giving living examples of faith. The work is always scrupulously researched and inclusive. They have made a tremendous contribution to RE in Reading.

ALFIE HAY, GENERAL ADVISER FOR EDUCATION TO READING BOROUGH COUNCIL

We asked one of our team coordinators, Sue Rees, to describe the session that she leads, which is most effective. Her response might surprise you.

The session 'Death, funerals and the Christian response' was written to respond to the request of one of our primary schools and is now being delivered in many others. During the session, pupils move through three workshops: 'exploring stages of grief', 'legacies' and 'eternal life'. This session has been extremely powerful. Pupils have amazed the team by how very open they are to sharing their own experiences, thoughts and feelings with us and their peers. They are respectful of each other's opinions, listening to and supporting one another. When they discuss the seven stages of grief, some have found that all the mixed emotions they have had are not unique, and that it's OK to feel them all—from sadness to anger. There is no need for guilt.

Teachers have been touched by listening to their pupils' feelings, bravely expressed to others. They have commented on the fact that children don't often get this opportunity at home, as we adults close up and won't talk about death. The pupils find themselves in a safe environment where they can share with each other.

When looking at and discussing legacies, pupils are asked, 'How would you like to be remembered?' and many change their views during the time, from 'being the best footballer', 'having lots of money' and so on to, for example, 'being kind to people'. The session makes them think and consider what is important to do with their lives now.

When thinking about life after death, they read the story *Waterbugs and Dragonflies*[1] in small groups. The story tells of a waterbug who watches all his friends climb the reeds and disappear, until one day he does the same and emerges into the air and beautiful light as a dragonfly. This illustrates for pupils how Christians believe they are on a journey here on earth, and that journey continues when we die. Like the dragonfly, we cannot go back down into the water to tell our friends how wonderful life is, but have to wait until they join us. The pupils discuss the themes of the story and then make a dragonfly each to help them to remember it.

SUE REES, REINSPIRED TEAM COORDINATOR

Well-designed sessions do more than simply deliver knowledge about Christianity. They provide opportunities to learn from

Christians, to consider the same issues that we consider, to come to their own conclusions and to engage more personally:

I've often found that the teaching material will elicit the pastoral concerns of the children. The REinspired approach doesn't just convey information, it actually allows for a pastoral response.

MARK LAYNE SMITH, CHAPLAIN AT READING UNIVERSITY AND REINSPIRED VOLUNTEER

Building a successful RE session has now been fashioned into a process, which our staff and, increasingly, others use to create their own, based on the needs of their individual schools, teachers and classes. We have around 50 session plans written up, with a variety of options and choices available to suit.

In this book we'll tell you the story of REinspired as we're going along. In Part Two we'll tell you more about how you can create your own RE sessions, but in Part One we'd like to introduce you to the key ideas that guide what we do and how we set about it.

If you feel inspired and want to have a go at supporting RE through your own church or want to form a local church partnership to do so, we'd like you to feel confident about it. If you'd like to come and see how we do it and chat to our staff and volunteers, please let us know. We run training courses which can help you get going, and we are also able to offer support in moving through the set-up stages of your own project. Please look at our website for more details.[1] You will also find there more information about materials and other resources, which can help you 'get it' and do something 'with it'.

Thinking further

- What excites you about this sort of approach to engaging with schools?

— Part One —

Getting it

*

— Chapter 1 —

From small beginnings

'What is God's kingdom like? ... It is like what happens when a mustard seed is planted in the ground. It is the smallest seed in all the world. But once it is planted, it grows larger than any garden plant.'

MARK 4:30–32

It is easy to forget how it felt to get that first primary RE session off the ground. Obviously, we were doing everything for the first time, but it was far more than that.

The invitation from the school to discuss a Christian input into RE needed a positive response. It had been long sought for but it was not what we were expecting in the last few days of the summer term. We could so easily have passed it by. When such openings are offered by schools, they need to be taken up positively. Teachers' school days are overflowing with demands. Churches need to spot the fact that, even in simply making contact, a teacher has made time for that in the full flow of school life. If you don't respond, he or she will give up, and the opening will probably pass and not return for a long time.

A number of factors might just lead you to let such an opportunity go by.

Feeling daunted

If you don't have experience of teaching in a school yourself, approaching the school, especially a senior member of staff, can feel daunting. You may not be familiar with the school's values or its ethos. You may be anxious about the sort of reception you will be given and uncertain about the expectations that will be made of you. You are probably not an expert in RE and may feel unsure about what you can offer. You are not alone.

A few years ago, I would never have thought I would be standing up at the front of a class, leading sessions. (I'm not an 'up front' person and I'm shy by nature.) If I had been asked to do this then, it would have been totally daunting. When I was asked to become a team coordinator, having been a volunteer for a couple of years, I felt prepared to take it on but with some trepidation. It was a privilege and honour to be involved in this exciting and valuable work. I still have a lot to learn, but I have a wonderful team to work with.

ALISON CHEVASSUT, REINSPIRED TEAM COORDINATOR

Distance and inertia

Often, relationships between local churches are polite but maintained at a distance. Going it alone can often feel like the easy option. Contemplating trying to work with people from other Christian traditions also involves crossing boundaries. There are differences in belief and understanding of Christian purpose, as well as the fact that we simply don't know each other that well. In addition, ecumenical relationships are often built up around united services and 'Churches Together' councils that are not necessarily oozing with energy, enthusiasm and cooperation for God's mission.

Busyness

The natural busyness of church life can easily become a barrier to the planting of a seed which will grow God's kingdom. Just contemplating a major initiative among schools, in addition to everything else, can make you feel exhausted, even if you are sitting in a well-upholstered recliner chair! It can leave you feeling overwhelmed before you have begun.

All of these barriers to beginning and responding are very real, but there are a number of helpful ideas that can take us through them.

Small can be very beautiful

To begin with, we worked on just one session at a time, only three in one school for the first year, and not many more in the next two years. At the time, we were often frustrated that the work didn't grow more quickly. Looking back, though, we can see that this slow development provided us with time to understand what we were attempting, time to explore more dynamic ways to prepare high-quality RE material and time to develop some strong educational practice. Starting small meant that working with other schools and increasing the number of RE sessions we delivered each year grew naturally out of the initial phase of the project. 'Quality before quantity' has become one of our governing principles as a result. So if you are considering supporting RE, we would actively encourage you to 'think small' to begin with. It is much more manageable.

From the beginning, think long term

The model we're describing is no short-term fix or 'hit and run' exercise. It aims at being both intentional and sustained, and it is a deeply relational approach. If, when you read this, you feel that you and your church are distanced from your local school's staff or your neighbouring churches, the chances are you'll also feel that this isn't how you would want it to be, in an ideal world. Supporting RE provides an extremely positive focus to help you change that position, but relationships need to be grounded in trust and understanding, and those qualities take time and ongoing commitment to build. A long-term view anticipates long-term outcomes for students, and long-term outcomes are more profound and bring greater opportunities than you could ever have imagined at the beginning.

You need to make a modest initial investment of time to pursue a particular aim. That investment may remain modest, but it can also grow in a way that can be managed, and healthy, active, trusting relationships with neighbouring schools and churches come as a wonderful byproduct.

Can someone else do this?

This is a great question, because the school will not be looking for you to become a teacher. They will be looking for their students to hear about the Christian faith 'from the inside'. In other words, they want Christians to be themselves within an education framework. You are the resource that the school needs as 'a person of faith'. In our approach, any Christian who is comfortable to be around children and enjoys the company of young people can play their part in it and experience the joy of appropriately sharing their faith among interested and enquiring students.

However, all our material is prepared so that others can join in and reshape it to use with another school. No one is indispensible. 'Replication' is an essential quality. It is always important that someone else can do the job as well. The result is that church leaders can quickly let others take their place with confidence, and, when an individual can no longer contribute to a team, the team will continue because another person can easily step in. The following example relates the experience of many 'ordinary church members'.

> *A just-retired couple from a local church, who have been faithful Christians all their lives, started volunteering by cutting out shapes and helping in craft activities. Over time, they grew in confidence such that they began to lead some of the small group work, which meant they had to do some personal preparation in order to get across to the children the ideas behind 'incarnation', 'baptism' and other such doctrinal words. They describe this process as 'the best Bible study ever'.*
>
> REVD DAN TYNDALL, VICAR OF ST PETER'S, CAVERSHAM

Some people will naturally find this kind of work easier than others. They will be better placed to make the first steps into school and approach other churches. Others will be pleased and excited to follow and to become a part of a school team that can allow the initiators to step back.

Start from where you are

What is important is to make a beginning. Maybe a direct approach needs to be made to a head teacher, but it is equally likely that either your church or another Christian community will have contact with the school through parents who could raise the issue of supporting RE through their child's teacher or the RE coordinator. Where a trusting relationship exists with a school, this may be a great place to begin a conversation.

Alternatively, ask your local RE coordinator whether they would welcome a gift to purchase new RE resources. In the early days of the project, we made such gifts to RE departments annually and were surprised to find that a gift of £50 might more than double the annual budget available to the RE coordinator in some schools to buy resources. This is a straightforward way to make a positive beginning in a relationship with your local school RE department.

It is easy for churches to become bogged down in talking about what might be achieved and how it can be done. The threat of a heavy set of meetings can bring the best initiative down and needs to be avoided. Keeping your administration and structures light, making your work focus on supporting the direct engagement of pupils, is most fruitful. Indeed, it is our repeated experience that we can explain the project to interested people but they have a 'conversion experience' when they see students enthusiastically engaged in exploring the Christian faith in RE. Getting an exploratory session or two underway is often a way of opening everyone's eyes to some wonderful outcomes.

Thinking further

- If you wanted to start an initiative like this, what issues would you need to overcome? Which of the strategies outlined above might be helpful?

— Chapter 2 —

Discovering that difference is great

Understanding the educational context

Often, 'church into school' projects adopt statements of faith for participating churches and volunteers to sign up to. These are often evangelical and can prove difficult for all Christian churches to agree with completely. However, as coordinators of a project that is supported by evangelical churches, we believe it is important to start by understanding what is important to the school.

This principle runs alongside other approaches to Christian mission. No one wishing to establish a project in another country would do so without taking time to understand the wishes, language and culture of the people among whom they were to work. Fresh Expressions of church in the UK[1] are springing up across the country, affirming the need for the 'culture of church' to be expressed in new ways within the different networks and contexts in which they are rooted. So when it comes to engaging with schools, it is critical to gain a good understanding of what is important to the school, to understand a bit about how it works and to overcome the myths that can often exist. In particular, it is important to understand the school's educational goals, the role of RE, how teachers hope that you will help them, and why, as local Christians, you might want to embrace this educational agenda. Here's some feedback from one of our local secondary schools.

Visiting speakers to schools must be able to communicate well with small and large groups of pupils, be aware of the learning needs of the children and recognise the purpose and objectives of RE. Not every faith representative can do this, so it is extremely valuable to have a group such as REinspired supporting us in recommending and preparing individuals to visit the school.

ANDY JOHNSON, HEAD OF RE AT MAIDEN ERLEGH SCHOOL

The national context

A new UK government took office in May 2010 and indicated that there would be some significant changes to education policy. In particular, the new planned primary curriculum was withdrawn, leaving the current guidance on RE appearing rather provisional. However, it seems unlikely that the important role of RE in the curriculum, which was reaffirmed in the 2010 guidance, will alter:

RE is an important curriculum subject. It is important in its own right and also makes a unique contribution to the spiritual, moral, social and cultural development of pupils and supports wider community cohesion. The Government is keen to ensure all pupils receive high-quality RE.[2]

RE has never been embraced in the National Curriculum and so is free of national targets and tests but it remains none the less a compulsory subject. Every pupil in a maintained school has an entitlement to religious education which is laid out in the 'Non-statutory National Framework for Religious Education'.[3]

The local context

What is taught in RE in your local school will be governed by a locally agreed syllabus, overseen by your local Standing Advisory Council on Religious Education (SACRE), on which local churches, along with other faith groups, will be represented.[4] The only exceptions to this are for voluntary aided church schools. You should be easily able to obtain a copy of the agreed syllabus from your local authority or school, and this is definitely the first thing to do. There you will find a detailed outline of what students in your local authority will be expected to learn and the significant place that Christianity normally has within the syllabus.

The law requires that every locally agreed syllabus must reflect that the religious traditions of Great Britain are in the main Christian whilst taking account of the teaching and practices of the other principal religions represented in Great Britain.[5]

'Learning about' and 'Learning from'

The 2004 Non-statutory Framework for RE identifies RE as having a significant role in promoting the spiritual, moral, social and cultural development of pupils.[6] There are two specific attainment goals in the teaching of RE, of 'Learning about' and Learning from' religions and their beliefs, which are understood as playing an essential role in achieving these wider aims.[7] Lat Blaylock, a leading RE adviser, explains the difference between these attainment goals as follows:

'Learning from' religion is school RE jargon in one way, but it carries a very helpful meaning for Christian contributors to RE as well. The idea is that you have not finished your RE if you have just collected a lot of facts. If you know your altar from your lectern, or your believer's baptism from your christening, then that might be interesting, or even useful. But RE offers a challenge, and a chance to think for yourself. This opportunity to learn from religion is like a window into faith. In fact, windows and doors are useful metaphors here. In church, Christians open the door to all, and invite them in to the community of Jesus. In school RE, a window into the faith is opened, so that you—or anyone—can have a really good look round and see what is going on. You don't

enter into the faith through the window, but the faith may challenge your own life, may open up new ideas.

So pupils learn about the Eucharist and remembering Jesus with bread and wine—then they consider whether remembering the past, or a person they love, is significant to them. They learn about gifts of gold and frankincense at Christmas, and consider whether they have gifts to give, and what it costs to give what we have to others. They learn about Jacob's ladder and the overwhelming sense of presence that he experienced that night, and they consider whether in dreams or visions they have ever wondered about a connection between earth and heaven. These are three of hundreds of possible ways of using the Christian tradition and the biblical narratives to explore the experiences and thoughts of children—that's learning from religion.[8]

When planning any input into RE, working with both these attainment goals is vital. Embracing the specific learning aims of each subject area in the syllabus makes your input relevant and significant to the teachers and students. You can add value to your input by including different approaches to learning, which support more general learning goals. Thinking imaginatively, you can contribute to other subject areas, such as literacy, numeracy and ICT capability, learning and thinking skills, appreciation of art, music and drama, and personal, social and emotional skills.

However, many primary teachers lack confidence in teaching RE. They may feel little personal empathy for teaching about faiths and beliefs. Try to imagine what issues might arise in your mind if you were asked not only to help students 'learn about' another religion but also to 'learn from' it.

To assist teachers at this point, the locally agreed syllabus will provide opportunities for 'people of faith' to be invited into schools to explain why they believe and what their faith means to them. There will also be a requirement on schools to visit local places of worship. It is in this 'curriculum space' that our approach is grounded.

Compare and contrast

A cursory dip into your local RE syllabus will quickly reveal that schools are interested in seeing a wide range of different expressions of Christian faith carefully articulated for their pupils rather than the presentation of only one. National guidance directs that 'RE has an important part to play as part of a broad, balanced and coherent curriculum'.[9]

Learning outside the classroom (LOtC) is recognised as important.[10] Visits to places of worship are specifically encouraged as examples of good practice.[11] The first visit that a school needs to arrange is often to enable pupils to 'contrast and compare' two different churches. This was the third session we arranged for our first school and is another good starting point.

The two nearest churches to that school were Baptist and United Reformed churches. Except that one had a baptistry and the other was cruciform in shape, we had to work hard to find differences. However, when we invited the local 'high' Anglican church (which also hosted our area's Greek Orthodox congregation) to join in, the educational task came alive in a dynamic and dramatic way. Moving from a simple, plain building with a pulpit, Communion table and a baptistry to a church that burnt incense, had a high altar and was full of icons made an unmistakable and instant impression and provoked the kind of inquisitive questioning that educationalists long for in students. The diversity of Christian expressions and beliefs, far from creating weakness or uncertainty, became the means of providing a high-value learning experience for pupils.

An understanding of the full breadth of Christian denominations is where the school's interest is focused and, consequently, opens up rich opportunities for Christian faith to be experienced and explored.

Thinking further

- What could you do to discover more about RE in your local school?
- What opportunities for high-value learning experiences could local churches easily create?

*

— Chapter 3 —

Respect

To an unknown God

When Paul looked around Athens, we read in the book of Acts that 'he was upset to see all the idols in the city'.[1] It was a multicultural city and an international centre of learning, full of different expressions of religious belief, none of them Christian. However, when Paul stood up to speak to the city council, he treated their beliefs with great respect, even though they caused him great distress. Why not read this passage in Acts 17:16–28 before you continue? It is noticeable that Paul didn't write off the Athenians' ideas or reject them out of hand but invested time in understanding where they were starting from. He began, 'People of Athens, I see that you are very religious…'[2]

Teaching pupils to respect beliefs other than their own is central to RE:

RE subject matter gives particular opportunities to promote an ethos of respect for others, challenge stereotypes and build understanding of other cultures and beliefs. This contributes to promoting a positive and inclusive school ethos that champions democratic values and human rights.

Indeed, it is perceived as making an important contribution to promoting community cohesion:

It provides a key context to develop young people's understanding and appreciation of diversity, to promote shared values and to challenge racism and discrimination. Effective RE will promote community cohesion.[3]

Addressing our own attitudes

It is easy to become critical of belief systems that differ from our own, and fail to deal with them respectfully. We often adopt such attitudes out of our ignorance rather than our knowledge of other beliefs and faiths.

During a sixth-form RE day, a Muslim visitor was asked what his response to the 9/11 attacks in the United States had been. He shattered all our expectations when he described the offence he had felt, knowing that these attacks had been undertaken in the name of Islam, and how he felt compelled by his faith to travel to New York with his own money to seek out and help victims of the attack on the Twin Towers of the World Trade Centre. I describe spirituality as what happens 'when the rubber (of our beliefs) meets the road (of life)'. When this visitor spoke of his spirituality, he opened our eyes to what most of us didn't know.

Whereas, in general, we may avoid encounters with people from other parts of society, one of the unique things about most schools is that we find every part of the surrounding community represented there. A community school is very much like the market place where Paul stood and spoke. It is where many other beliefs and world views are encountered and exchanged. To be allowed to contribute to the learning of a school is an important privilege, which needs to be highly valued, and we do well to invest in understanding other faiths in order to be properly prepared.

Being open-hearted

Paul found that he was not easily understood. His ideas seemed alien to the Athenians. 'People were asking, "What is this know-all trying to say?"'[4]

Adopting an open-hearted and respectful attitude, being

prepared to listen and learn from others so that they in turn may listen and learn from us, seems fundamental to the good critical engagement that is central to education and RE. So, whenever there is an opportunity to acknowledge another faith in a session on Christianity, we do so. For instance, if we look at pictures of Jerusalem, we include pictures of the Dome of the Rock and the western wall of the temple and acknowledge that it is an important city to Jews and Muslims as well as Christians. If we are asked to lead a session on why Christians go on pilgrimage, we will refer to the pilgrimages of other faiths. The use of holy writings, prayers and festivals are other obvious touch-points.

It is also a strong Christian position to 'model difference', by extending to Christians of other denominations and people of other faiths or none the freedom to share what they believe in front of students. At the end of the day, it will be for students to explore and find out what they themselves believe.

RE encourages pupils to learn from different religions, beliefs, values and traditions while exploring their own beliefs and questions of meaning. It challenges pupils to reflect on, consider, analyse, interpret and evaluate issues of truth, belief, faith and ethics and to communicate their responses.[5]

It is vital for a school to be confident that their visitors are able to understand how to walk this path. If this can be done appropriately, it becomes an additional reason for them to draw you into school. It also means that when you engage students, you are more likely to be sensitive to starting from where they are in their thinking.

What to avoid

It is important to note that 'Religious Education (RE) should be taught in an objective and pluralistic manner, and not as indoctrination into a particular faith or belief'.[6] Historically, this hasn't always been the case, but the church must be alert to the fact that schools have changed and the language of 'proclamation' and 'confession' which is the staple of church life on a Sunday is not appropriate or acceptable in school from Monday to Friday.

If this is the guidance given to schools, it should not surprise Christian visitors to schools, if they stray into a 'confessional' approach, that they are not invited back again. If the invitation into school is made on the basis of an 'objective and pluralistic' approach, it is not honest or Christian to subvert that arrangement. Respect for Christ's name should keep us from this error. (Further discussion on this issue will be found in the next chapter.)

How to speak of Jesus

In this narrative from Acts, which has often been used to help Christians think about how to share Christian faith in another culture, Paul famously found a different way to tell the Jesus story.

'As I was going through your city and looking at the things you worship, I found an altar with the words, "To an unknown God." You worship this God, but you don't really know him. So I want to tell you about him.' [7]

Preaching to tell others what they should believe, in an exclusive way, is a frequent part of our approach in church, but it is not the only way of speaking powerfully about the gospel. In school, it is also possible to use proclamation to set the Christian story alongside the distinctive beliefs and worldviews of students. This can be done through the language of testimony, giving an account of your personal belief and why you believe it, rather than an instruction to others about what they should believe. Of course, experience tells us that when someone shares why they believe, it is likely to be a profound event for the listener, but then RE is not intended to be an arid discussion of religion but a subject filled with meaning.

We start every session we lead by saying, 'We are not here to change what you believe but to tell you about what Christians believe.' Prefacing our next words with 'I believe…' or 'A Christian might believe…' is the key to achieving this aim.

No better opportunity

One of our schools invited us to lead a session on 'Prayer' for Year 6. They thought they would do the job properly so they asked the children to write questions for us to address. The result was 60 sets of questions not just on prayer but on a wide range of spiritual issues and concerns, which were all at the heart of the RE curriculum.

Religious education provokes challenging questions about the ultimate meaning and purpose of life, beliefs about God, the self and the nature of reality, issues of right and wrong, and what it means to be human.[8]

The school felt overwhelmed by their pupils' response and asked us to return to run a session that addressed these additional issues. Confronted by questions about the origins of the world, the nature of suffering, Christian beliefs about God and what happens to us when we die, we set up opportunities within a session for pupils to ask their own questions in small groups. To be given the opportunity to sit and answer students' questions about what I believe about death and my hope of heaven, and to offer my perspectives on personal doubts, questions and experiences of loss was a tremendous privilege and an opportunity to share faith in school that I have rarely seen surpassed. The fact that this session is now one of those most frequently requested by schools is evidence of the widespread spiritual needs that students in primary schools are already urgently seeking to address.

Thinking further

- How does this vision of engagement fit with yours? Does it sound like a compromise or an opportunity?
- Do you have any relationships with people of other faiths that might offer a way to personalise and deepen your understanding of their beliefs?

※

— Chapter 4 —

'E' is for education

If a church relates to a school with an agenda that goes beyond the support of education, the danger is that, at some point, the additional agenda will become apparent. As soon as that happens, the trust that has been built up, probably over a long period of time, will almost certainly be lost. Sadly, there are too many schools who feel they cannot trust their local churches to keep within the educational framework.

Nevertheless, for some Christians, access to schools presents itself as an opportunity for evangelism, not education. REinspired does not believe that evangelism is a bad thing or that Christians should never confront others with the truth of the gospel of Jesus: the opposite would be the case. It is simply that as a visitor to school, it is not appropriate to engage in evangelism. More importantly, 'evangelism' is not necessarily the most effective way of communicating faith.

In RE, students are invited to analyse and criticise different faith beliefs and to question deeply, so that (to use a computing analogy) they can 'download' what they find significant for themselves at any point. As is so often the case with Internet use, the 'downloading' of information is very much within the student's control, and the observer can't always know if it has taken place. However, sometimes it becomes clear that 'downloading' has occurred, as it is spontaneously expressed by the student.

There was one occasion when a school was visiting a Baptist church to 'contrast and compare' the building with another from a different denomination. Around the church were different members of the team, running 'stations' that groups of pupils would visit. There were stations exploring church activities, discovering the special services that were held in the church, finding out about the history of the church, learning about the Lord's Supper, reading from the big pulpit Bible, inspecting the baptistry and asking about believer's baptism. When one Afro-Caribbean boy arrived at the last base, having read from the pulpit and listened to the explanation about the baptistry, he confidently announced in front of his teacher and his friends, 'One day I want to get in there.'

Other students have gone home after sessions and challenged their parents about why they say they are Christians but don't go to church, with the result that whole families have begun to attend. Others have headed round to an Anglican church after school, asking to be baptised. These are the occasions that staff and volunteers frequently remember, but in every session pupils are drawing down for themselves positive impressions of the Christian faith, truths that may shape their lives, ways of understanding and responding to the world about them, and a tangible understanding of what can be believed about God.

Honesty, please!

Of course, it is very easy for misunderstandings to arise about the agenda of the church in supporting RE. We seek to avoid these in a number of ways.

Firstly, we seek to maintain a clear focus. In the early days of REinspired, we engaged in a range of activities as well as leading RE and collective worship, which included an after-school roadshow and an after-school club. These approaches both had their place, but we have chosen to confine ourselves to supporting RE and collective worship as our Trust's main areas of work, to avoid any sense of confusion.

Secondly, seeking strong feedback is an essential task for us. We work hard to build good relationships with teachers. Every session's content is negotiated and approved with teachers in advance, to ensure that it is on track to address their educational goals and they are happy with its content and methodology. Afterwards we insist that they give us their criticism, so that we can be aware of any issues next time around or can talk through with them anything we need to understand better. It is very easy to leave with less than honest comments. If this does occur, not only do we remain unaware of vital feedback but, if something didn't go well from the school's point of view, the teacher may become reluctant to use the project's services in future. Strong feedback can save us from our worst mistakes.

It can be hard to hear criticism when we have put in so much effort, but it is an opportunity to amend and refine what we offer our schools. Often, the strongest and most immediate criticism comes from our volunteers when they tell us what has or hasn't worked for them or the children. The teacher's feedback tells us the session's strengths and weaknesses and whether or not the material has been delivered successfully. It is important to value the good and the bad, to follow up on any concerns and amend them, so that mistakes are not repeated. This helps us build relationship and find out where the boundaries really are.

Sometimes feedback can be about practical things, like safety. This teaches us not to be complacent. One of our sessions used the image of father and family to illustrate God and church. The teacher pointed out that many in her class didn't have a father figure at home and family life was difficult at best. It was a poignant reminder that we mustn't take anything for granted.

JULIA JONES, REINSPIRED TEAM COORDINATOR

Thirdly, we insist that, in any correspondence, there is only one message being given to both church and school. We have only one set of aims laid out, in one foundational document for the Trust, so it is clear to both church and school that there are absolutely no hidden agendas around evangelism in particular.

Our written aim is 'Enabling schools and their pupils to develop spiritually and engage creatively with faith'. To the Christian keen to share their faith, this might sound limited, but limiting the 'territory' in which we work to the educational agenda has proved to be powerful. We would maintain that the greater our transparency, the greater the trust that schools will offer to us.

Working among other faiths

Working in the unique community of a school, in which every part of a local community is represented, means exercising a lot of sensitivity. There is a parental right of withdrawal from RE and, if this right was taken up to any significant degree, our input would become divisive. Conversely, if all parents are confident that RE sessions will be appropriately delivered, the school's confidence in the church team will quickly grow.

One excellent test to apply to your plans is to ask this question. How would you feel if you had a child who visited another faith's place of worship with the school, and the child was presented with material from that faith in the way that you are planning to present Christian material? If you're not happy about that thought, you nearly always need to think again and plan differently.

Working with other faiths

We are not in a position to support RE by helping with teaching about other faiths from the inside. However, we do work with people of other faiths to help them to engage in comparable ways with RE. In particular, we recognise that for some schools, in ethnically mixed communities, it is vital for them to offer a 'balance' to our external input from some of the other faiths.

It is very important for schools to listen to parents' and, sometimes, governors' concerns. As input into RE developed in one school, comments were made about the number of visits being made by students to churches, and we were asked to move some of the sessions into school. Often, such decisions are not made in discussion with the Trust. For this school, we invested time with the local authority's RE adviser, to work with local Muslims to establish a team that still delivers two sessions for the school in appropriate and helpful ways for the students. One session involves a visit to a mosque and the second a visit by local Muslims to the school to talk about the five pillars of Islam.

When Jesus is unnamed

Much of this book will focus on supporting schools in contexts where Jesus is 'named'. However, when we are engaged in schools but Jesus remains 'unnamed', this doesn't mean that he is not seen in what happens there. On the contrary, often it is when we act in a distinctively Christian way in school, especially when encountering other beliefs, that our faith is authenticated.

A challenging paradox

As students grow older, in secondary school, there are many occasions when we work alongside people from other faiths in a variety of contexts, including RE and collective worship. This models the tolerance and inclusivity that are sought in the curriculum and are vital to community cohesion in the school. Razwan Ul Haq is a Sufi Muslim artist and educational adviser who works with schools across the UK.[1] We asked him to reflect on the day he spent with us in a sixth form recently.

In today's Britain, where there is a general reluctance to talk about religions in schools, it is really important to present religious experience in a positive way. I believe we help counter negative stereotypes about religions when we work together. By bringing Muslim and Christian faiths into the classroom, sixth-form pupils were able to have a firsthand experience of practitioners. Schools need spirituality and the myth that 'religion' is devoid of spirituality can be debunked when pupils see spirituality on the face of religious people. Also, bringing in faith practitioners provides a moral dimension and allows pupils to access the richness of life.

However, working as a Christian in partnership with someone of another faith also reveals a challenging paradox. We find that, for students approaching the end of their school careers, their engagement with the Christian gospel is greatest when it is offered alongside the views of people of other faiths and none. Students may reject ideas if they are 'handed down' but enjoy being challenged to make a critical assessment of different views. They aspire to be approached in an adult way and find it helpful to experience people of different faiths modelling their differences positively. We find that the gospel stands up well in this context. When presented alongside a wide variety of views, it can be most easily seen and received.

Thinking further

- How would you react to honest feedback if it was offered?
- Is having confidence in the gospel enough?
- 'Named or unnamed, Christ is present.' What is the impact of believing this in the way we might work in schools?

— Chapter 5 —

Aiming high and building strong

United we stand

One of the great strengths of the REinspired model is that it recognises the vital role that every Christian tradition has to play in supporting RE. Each one is respected and valued. It is therefore a good way to draw together even quite disparate churches to offer a valuable visible expression of Christian unity. This was something we didn't plan but just discovered as we went along. However, for those who visit the project, it is an aspect that often leaves the strongest impressions.

Christian unity also came to be a great way of underpinning our foundational goal. We aim to see 'every student in every school at least once a year for RE, ideally in one of our churches'. We have yet to achieve that goal, but we do currently engage 83 per cent of all primary students in eleven schools every year. In some schools we've been working with 100 per cent for some time and seeing some pupils more than once a year.

It isn't necessary to start with such a large goal, and to work with just one school is fine. We certainly didn't set out with such a large vision, but there is strength in working systematically with pupils in each year of their primary career. Once we'd found that this was a way of engaging schools that was welcomed by teachers, the possibility of re-engaging with young people across our community with our beliefs, places of worship and congregations seemed an excellent aspirational target.

To contemplate such an aim, a lot of people need to get involved. If you start to follow such a vision, you will quickly realise that you need to mobilise every church to contribute people, buildings and resources. It is undoubtedly a case of 'all hands on deck'. Although not every church can always offer everything, every contribution is welcome.

It is helpful to remember that if you want to aim high, the development required to support your aims will not need to happen all at once. Indeed, churches and volunteers come on board at different speeds and in different ways, and their contributions can develop over time. It would also be true to say that there are never enough volunteers and it is unlikely that there ever will be. The nature of the project is that, once it has momentum, it extends ahead of its capacity. Knowing the direction in which to steer it is one of the key roles of its leaders. Living with the experience of stretched resources is fairly normal. The project needs careful management but should also remind you of how growth will usually feel in this part of God's kingdom.

It's not my school!

At a fairly early point, churches have to learn to relinquish any strong sense of ownership about particular schools. In some places, we hear stories of churches competing to work with a school to the exclusion of other Christians. To maximise the input and impact that churches can make together, we have to relax and trust each other enough to work collaboratively. Recognising that schools work is for the building of the kingdom of God, as much as for the growth of the church, is an excellent way to begin to look at the issue. In eternity we hope that our church denominations will be lost but that the kingdom of God will be recognised and established. Behaving as if it will be otherwise is sheer foolishness.

The story of REinspired

Building a team

The building of our primary school teams has happened in different ways. We aim to offer support in RE to every local primary school and, over time, the schools have steadily taken up that offer. After a few years, our first team was strong enough to divide in two, and each team began to serve a different school. Subsequently, each of those teams served a second school as well. We asked Pete Stone, one of our team leaders at that time, to reflect on this stage of our development.

We had new opportunities, but could we fulfil them? We asked our current volunteers to take on one or two extra sessions to get us going, which they did, and then often found the capacity to stay on. We asked them if they knew any mums who went to their church and whose children attended the school we had now been invited into. This was a great source of volunteers. Also the clergy of nearby churches got involved and brought with them older people with experience and skills. They then promoted the lessons in their churches, which drew others in. But it was always a 'tightrope walk', finding volunteers, helping them understand our ethos and enabling them find their place in the team in order to resource new sessions.

Initially, team members came from local churches but we were contacted early on by parents who were keen to be involved. They lived outside our area and worshipped at other churches but their children attended the schools we served. Some schools had small prayer groups who would pray for us, and sometimes their members would become involved. However, there is probably no substitute for parents chatting in the playground at the end of the school day to help recruitment of new volunteers to the teams.

Team members vary enormously. Not only are they likely to have varied Christian experience and denominational allegiance, but they will also be at different stages of life. Many retired people find that they have time to offer. Some will enjoy helping out around the children and may have additional time to help prepare craft materials. Others may be keen to take on a leading role and are looking for more substantial challenges. There are parents who are taking time out of work, and among them there may well be some teachers who can bring a special contribution. In most churches, there are people engaged in working with primary aged children who are willing to make time available for this sort of initiative. Many members of the church staff are also pleased to assist when available. Sue Rees, one of our team coordinators, offers some of her hot tips for involving new people in her teams.

I have found that one of the best ways of recruiting volunteers to help with REinspired sessions is by spending time enthusing about the project with people, whether in local churches or in the playground. Most importantly, then, I invite them along to see a lesson in practice. This way, they not only get excited about what we are doing in schools but get 'hooked'. Building relationships with volunteers is as important as building relationships with the schools.

Sometimes we have approached a particular group of churches to come up with both people and modest financial resources to support a team in one or more of their local schools, and this has become a challenge to which they can respond effectively.

Team coordinators

Each of our teams has been led by a 'team coordinator', sometimes two working together. To start with, these people always gave their time on a voluntary basis. More recently, we have begun to pay them, to secure their involvement, ensure professional standards and develop accountability. A minority have been staff on church teams. Usually they are people with a range of gifts. We would expect them to be good administrators, with a capacity to develop a team, and an ability to develop materials with others and ultimately to lead a session from the front when required. All our team leaders have been very different, but they all have a 'chemistry' that communicates with the pupils and an ability to relate to the staff at their teams' schools.

Securing strong relationships with schools

At the beginning of the project, two members of the team always visited the teachers in person, first to negotiate a session and then again afterwards to review it. Establishing a good understanding and a rapport is time well spent and an essential long-term investment. Often, it can be a frustrating process. Teachers are notoriously busy and are not easily accessible by phone at school. Email has become an important way of communicating, but it isn't a substitute for sitting down face to face. Ensuring that the teachers are happy with the sessions means that the Trust's work retains a place in the school's pattern of work for the following academic year.

Where the relationship with a school is held through only one or two people, it will always be vulnerable to changes in personnel on both sides. However, the REinspired model intentionally seeks to build wide and deep relational links into school, and this aim is structurally included in our pattern of work.

The effectiveness of this approach came home to us when the head teacher of a local school retired, the deputy was taken seriously ill and the RE coordinator moved to a new school. In addition, our team coordinator changed. Most relationships with schools would have stalled at this point. However, as every teacher apart from the head teacher had taken part in our sessions, it was simply agreed that we would work with the same programme that we had offered the previous academic year.

Joy and laughter

Working ecumenically, while respecting each other's traditions, inevitably throws up some fantastic opportunities and some hilarious situations.

One of the extremely enriching outcomes of working together with people from other churches is a breaking down of our ignorance about each other's beliefs and practices. On the occasion of our first ever school's work session, a woman from a Catholic church was part of the team. She had never witnessed an act of believer's baptism before, but the effect on her was profound.

I enjoyed my first session very much and, ever since, I have been involved whenever I can. It included my first experience of believer's baptism as it happens in a Baptist church. It reminded me of the Bible and I pictured Jesus and John the Baptist in the River Jordan. It was a lovely feeling, taking some of the children into the empty baptistry in later sessions.

MEL NORONHA, REINSPIRED VOLUNTEER

Mel is still a team member and still discovering. There have been other wonderful occasions when the same team has had the privilege of being introduced to the burning of incense in a 'high' Anglican church and the amazing beauty of Greek Orthodox iconography.

However, in a school led operation, from time to time the wonderfully bizarre can also take place. In offering respect to other people's faith perspectives, we agree to offer respect to each other in the explanation of each other's beliefs. A Baptist might easily find him- or herself sharing how some churches christen children, while an Anglican might equally explain believer's baptism. Sometimes, though, even stranger things occur.

Pete Stone recalls an incident from his time as REinspired's Project Manager.

The lesson that afternoon was going to look at both infant and adult baptism with 60 five and six-year-olds. I was going to do the adult / believer's baptism bit, but then I got a phone call to say that the vicar who was going to demonstrate the infant baptism was needed elsewhere. To add to this, Trinity Church, where we were going to do the lesson, was undergoing building work. We could still use their font but the lesson would now take place in the Salvation Army church. OK, not to panic—we are adaptable in REinspired! However, when we arrived at the Salvation Army, many issues came to my mind. I was thinking, 'I was only doing the adult / believer's baptism talk, and now I'm doing the infant baptism demonstration. But I'm a dyed-in-the-wool full immersion baptiser. What's going on? I've got to carry a font across ASDA's car park, and we are doing a talk about baptism in the Salvation Army church, which doesn't practise baptism. What a crazy world!' But as I did not get struck by lightning while crossing the car park carrying the font and the children got a wonderful insight into what Christians believe about baptism, we must have been doing something right!

Thinking further

- Who do you know who would be interested to be part of a team?
- Whose support do you need to seek if you are to make a beginning?

— Chapter 6 —

Partnership

The REinspired project has developed a principle of 'partnership' to underpin our activity. Churches, volunteers, individual donors and trusts, schools, a local education authority and other faith groups have all partnered us formally or informally. This has become a way of describing the relationship we have through our shared concern to support RE in schools.

Church partners

The project started out being supported by a dozen churches but today we are grateful for the participation of 22 church partners. They may commit to pray for us, support the project financially, offer volunteers to staff or advise the project, or simply lend us their premises.

However, it would be a mistake to think that REinspired seeks to engage across an ever-increasing number of schools. One of the key principles is that local churches need to be relating to local schools. We recognise that we can only do that effectively for schools in our 'parish', which, for the sake of convenience, is defined by the geographical boundaries of our four Anglican parishes. This area includes eleven primary schools and two secondary schools. This year, a school for students with special needs has been opened as well.

Most of the churches in our area have been or are currently directly involved. The situation of churches can change, and there is a continual need for the project to be reconnecting with them to keep them up to date with new developments and challenges and to thank them and offer appreciation of their support. This ongoing connection is hard to sustain in a project that seeks to respond positively to opportunities offered by the schools, but it is nonetheless an essential task.

To help us to keep up, we have started to build a team of REinspired Advocates in each of the churches. Resourced from the project, their task is to keep the profile of the project high in their fellowships, communicating important information to church leaders and congregations.

Individual partners

The project would go nowhere without the 80 volunteers who currently support the RE sessions, but there is a wider group that includes, among others, housebound elderly people who pray and/or give time and money to support it. Every partner will receive a newsletter three times a year, telling them what's going on. There's a prayer diary that lets them know about requests for prayer, including those that are made by schools.

School partners

We have always wanted to transform the sort of relationship we have with schools. Entering schools as a 'religious visitor', it is possible to feel that staff members are treating us circumspectly, as if we are 'someone who might do something we will all regret'. We are eager to be accepted and trusted as part of a wider team by schools and teachers, to be seen as people who can be relied on to deliver what the school needs. So we talk to schools about partnership, which describes the relationship we continually aspire to be offered by them.

After discussions with local primary head teachers, we wrote to them inviting their schools to formalise their relationship with the project and become not just partners but 'contributing partners'. Some schools have come to view us as an invaluable part of their teaching programme. They couldn't afford to 'buy us in' at full cost; nor would we be prepared to offer our sessions as anything other than a gift from the churches. However, some have signed up to contribute several hundred pounds each year to the cost of the sessions delivered in their schools, to help us take the project forward and to acknowledge the different relationship in which we now find ourselves.

Alan Youd is the head teacher of Hawkedon Primary School and reflects on the relationship that REinspired has developed with the school.

In my experience as a young person growing up in a C of E local church community in the late 1950s and 1960s, the congregation spent a great deal of time discussing what others were wearing rather than how they were working towards developing a better community. In my teaching career I have also encountered ministers whose sole purpose was to recruit to the church and to insist that all children must follow the doctrines and traditions of the church.

It was therefore a great relief, when I first came to Lower Earley in April 1997, to find that the churches worked together for the community. Unfortunately, my first experience of this was on my very first day as Head of Hawkedon, when a Year 5 pupil was killed by a hit-and-run driver. It was then that I saw the churches working together for the family concerned and the school. Therefore, when REinspired was created, I knew that those involved had already worked out a positive relationship and that they wanted to work with the schools in whatever capacity they could for the spiritual benefit of all the local community.

Over the years, we have worked closely, using everyone's unique experience and skills to formulate an understanding and working relationship which means that we share the same goals and aspirations, as well as sharing the resources and capabilities of our different organisations.

My advice to any school which may have an opportunity to develop a similar relationship is that, with cooperation and understanding, anything is achievable.

Partnering other faiths

In working with other faiths, our aim has never been to lose the distinctiveness of our own beliefs. However, we are concerned to recognise that, for teachers, faith can be a cause of anxiety, especially where there is the potential for tension in the school community. Historically, we have not been able to go into some schools because of this anxiety. We felt that we needed to have some purchase on this critical issue so that we could avoid being part of the problem and begin to become part of the solution.

In addition, in our secondary school work it has often been useful to have different voices in RE and collective worship, reflecting the make-up of the student community. At one point we succeeded in working with Year 12 and 13 teaching staff, a Muslim leader and the Jewish Rabbi to plan and deliver a scheme of work through the year. This has allowed for a stronger presentation of distinctive Christian beliefs alongside other religious views, and has highlighted the way in which treating older teenagers in a more adult fashion facilitates their deeper engagement.

Such partnerships come and go with the changes in personnel. Working to maintain wide relationships can be demanding on time as they constantly have to be renewed. However, this is always an invaluable gift to be able to offer a school, and a few years ago we were encouraged when the local Muslim Council decided it was happy to work alongside us in this way.

The annual bash

Every year we have some sort of gathering to which we invite all our partners, including those who fund us as well as others who work with us in the local authorities and local SACREs. The local authorities offer a crucial relationship and, where confidence can be built, have been able to facilitate the use of public premises and opportunities to meet other staff and deliver training.

At these annual events, we often move away from formal business. We try to present some of the innovative areas of our practice or to draw in someone from outside to train, entertain and envision, such as in the art of Christian storytelling in school. It is our way of keeping in touch, of building understanding among all our partners and expressing our profound thanks to them.

Thinking further

- What would help you to build stronger relationships with schools?

— Chapter 7 —

Hot tips!

Persistence, patience and prayer

Often, overtures to churches, schools, prospective volunteers and other potential partners don't result in the immediate positive responses you anticipated. It is easy to be disappointed or even despairing when, yet again, what seems obvious to you doesn't 'drop', like the proverbial penny, in the mind of the person you are approaching. It is therefore important to keep the long view in mind and to remember that you are engaged in a spiritual exercise.

A hundred years ago, churches were at the heart of education in the UK as initiators and providers. Over the decades, that position has diminished. More recently, though, there have been an increasing number of projects and church workers around the UK committed to offering input to schools. If the church is no longer represented in a school, it doesn't mean that God is no longer present and active there.

It is easy to forget that many Christian teachers see their job as a vocation, and recent initiatives such as 'Transforming Lives' have sought to encourage more Christians to explore this calling.[1] This is especially true of RE specialists.

God is ever present and active and, as visitors to schools, we need to look out for the opportunities he will give us to support the work he is already doing there. If the openings we seek don't immediately materialise, we must be prepared to listen deeply to the explanations given. People may have held a different vision in the past of what schools work is about, and it may take time for them to understand another vision for engaging schools. Be open to the possibility that, as you pray and trust God for the journey, the people you least expect to get involved will do just that, 'out of the blue'. As Paul writes, 'What can we say about all this? If God is on our side, can anyone be against us?'[2]

If you are thinking about taking an initiative in schools like the one we describe, here are four other hot tips that we would commend to you.

1) Always develop good practice

One of the outcomes that emerged when we started delivering RE sessions in churches, rather than in the classroom, was the freedom to think afresh and in new ways. There are many 'schemes of work' in schools that suffer from being repeated and not refreshed.

At the beginning, the move from school to church opened up all sorts of creative opportunities to offer a vivid view of faith for students to see. The sessions had an 'experiential feel': students would always be 'hands on', they undertook their learning alongside interesting new adults, and there were always new places to visit and unexpected things to look at, encounter and explore.

As we move forward, these experiences still stay fresh for students, but we aim to keep innovating at each level of our work. Every year, in every session, it is healthy to identify a minimum of one area where you want to innovate, experiment, improve or alter. The educational aims remain the same but the delivery and the material need to be constantly reviewed and renewed. This needn't mean expending much additional time; it's just about adopting a different approach. But it keeps the sessions fresh and the practice at its best, and that is always what counts.

2) Build up a portfolio of skills

In the same way, it is good to look for a variety of ways of achieving your aims. Some of our staff explored the possibilities of incorporating an approach and skills based on the methodology of Godly Play,[3] to great effect. We find that this method works well particularly with younger pupils in smaller groups.

More recently, we have had a tremendous amount of fun learning from Bob Hartman about telling Christian stories in creative and engaging ways. It's easy to pick up, is relevant in all sorts of situations and is a great way to equip lots of the volunteers to enliven their storytelling.[4]

Three years ago, local head teachers asked us whether we could put on an event to help Year 6 pupils adjust to moving up to secondary school. We wanted to be able to respond to the need they identified. We now run an annual 'transition event'. It involves clips from the television programme *Top Gear*, the hire of the local leisure centre, and the creation of an opportunity for up to 400 pupils from across the primary schools to experience their new peer groups at secondary school and begin to establish new relationships.

The 'You say goodbye, I say hello' event is a wonderful opportunity for our Year 6 pupils to meet new classmates and, I know, helps the less confident ones to begin to feel that, actually, moving on to secondary school will be an exciting challenge, not a threat.

STEVE SCOTT, HEAD TEACHER OF EARLEY ST PETER'S PRIMARY SCHOOL

This event also allows us to say goodbye to children after working with them for six years and let them know that we'll be seeing them again in Year 7, if they are moving to a local school. When we ask students, 'What was the best bit?' they almost universally answer the same way:

Meeting others going to my school.

I liked getting to know people at my new school best… when we were finding out things about other people.

Well, I've come across some of them, but it's nice to meet some different ones to get to know them.

As confident relationships with a school grow, all sorts of requests for your input may arise. The development of a sacred space in school, offering pastoral support for staff, or one-to-one work with children have all been requested. Knowing which avenue to pursue is important to staying on track. However, we have always been concerned to keep the exploration of the Christian faith within RE as the primary focus of our work, while remaining alert to requests that other church groups might be able to address.

3) Encourage your volunteers and staff

Developing a culture in which everyone's point of view matters is a good starting point. Many sessions start with a team meeting over lunch, followed by a read-through of the session to answer any concerns and to instil confidence. Afterwards, over a cup of tea, there is always a review of how things went, in which everyone's views will be noted and appreciated.

If you are a project leader, it is easy to stick with doing the same things yourself, but the best thing you can do is to encourage others to develop into new roles and to work your way out of a job. We have realised that it is positive and healthy to encourage volunteers and staff to aspire to be stretched and to grow. This has frequently resulted in a positive step change in the resources we can offer.

4) Keep the evidence

In case someone asks you or your school for evidence of positive learning, it is always good to have it carefully kept. Collect any sort of evidence of the quality of your students' reactions and the impact your contribution is having on their thinking. We try to provide space for students to reflect on what's been important in a session, and then to write, draw or find some other way of recording it for later. Often, this evidence will be in the form of worksheets, which can reinforce learning but will be retained by the school. Sometimes schools will encourage pupils to write to express their thanks and tell us what the session has meant to them, and these comments are nearly always most meaningful. Here are some from four Year 6 pupils in a multicultural school after attending a session about Christmas.

I am a Muslim… When I first went to a church I didn't know much about it and I didn't understand it. When you and the helpers had spoken about it I understood it perfectly because you had explained it so well… Last Monday it was our Muslim Eid. We sort of celebrate it in the same way as Christians celebrate Christmas—we both give presents.

ZANUB

Even though I'm not a Christian, I think it is important to know about other people's religions… I can't believe Mary was only 14 when the angel came to visit her. She must have been very worried Joseph wouldn't marry her any more… Even though we've been to the church before, we never do the same activities!

LUCY

When I entered the door I knew it was going to be exciting. When I looked up in the church it felt like Noah's ark because of the roof… When Rob told us about the nativity story in three parts, I was dying to find out more.

MALENSU

You rock! You opened my eyes to so many beautiful things. When I grow up to be a well-practised Christian, people will ask me how I do it and I shall say all the credit is owed to REinspired.

MARTHA

Hot tips!

Seeing is believing

When someone new to the project needs an explanation of what happens in the sessions, a verbal account is no substitute for a personal encounter. Inviting people to come and see enables them to experience the positive learning and dynamic encounters that are commonplace in every session. When people ask to visit the project, we always let them choose the session they would like to attend, confident that they will be excited and envisioned, whatever the subject or venue might be. Kathryn Morgan, who is a Mission Adviser to the Baptist Union, describes her experience.

Arriving at a modern church building in Reading, I was welcomed into a team meeting and quickly discovered that I was not going to succeed in the mental game of 'Spot the Anglican, Methodist and so on', because this was a well-integrated team from a wide range of churchmanship, happy to work together as Christians. We moved into a time of preparation for the afternoon, with the difficult theme of 'death and bereavement', so that when 62 children arrived with their teachers and helpers, everything was in place.

The next hour and a half was a revelation to me! After the standard welcome and explanation about not trying to change anyone's beliefs but explaining Christian understanding, there was a good introduction about funerals and then the children split into groups. As I sat in on each of the three activities experienced by each group, I observed them to be superbly prepared and sensitively run. The children were attentive and thoughtful, sharing experiences and asking meaningful questions. Some related feelings where their young lives had already been affected by the death of someone close to them. From each activity, each child took away a craft or written expression of their own thoughts, making up a personal recollection of the afternoon.

Coming back together to watch a relevant DVD clip from The Lord of the Rings, *the questions that the children asked revealed how effective the input had been in opening up the subject and provided an easy opening to speak of the Christian understanding of salvation and heaven.*

In general, whether it is about engaging a church, recruiting a volunteer, gaining the support of a Trust or securing the support of an Education Department, a visit is what excites people the most.

Thinking further

- What questions do you still have? What would you like to understand more?
- Would seeing the REinspired practice in action help you?

— Part Two —

Doing something with it

*

— Chapter 8 —

Creating a session (1)

REinspired has really helped me to deliver the RE syllabus in school. One afternoon can cover a large part of a topic and either be the starting point for work in school or a reinforcement in a practical way for the work done in school. A big plus is how much the children enjoy it.

JANET WHITEMAN, RE COORDINATOR, RADSTOCK PRIMARY SCHOOL

Imagine that the RE coordinator from your local primary school has asked you to run a session on Jesus' parables for six- to seven-year-olds. Sixty children, accompanied by their teachers and other adults, are coming to your church for an hour's session. Where do you start?

The locally agreed RE syllabus

First stop is the locally agreed RE syllabus. The school's RE coordinator will have a copy they can lend you but you'll want to obtain your own from the SACRE through the local authority. Alternatively, if you are working with a church voluntary aided school, they will have their own syllabus. This is your handbook. Even if you know the parables, their theology and their application inside out, you still need to know what the children are required to learn. Many local syllabuses work by asking similar questions about each faith. So you'll probably find questions like these for Christianity at Key Stage One that might be relevant:

- What did Jesus teach people about God?
- What stories did Jesus tell and why did he tell them?
- How do Christians believe they should treat other people?

- What do Christians believe about how people should live with others?
- What do Christians believe makes a person special?

A creative conversation

A good way to start is to get your volunteers together over coffee. After praying that God would help and inspire, encourage each person to offer all of their creative ideas to the challenge of thinking 'outside the box' and exploring the subject from the child's perspective. The conversation might go something like this:

'We've got to plan a new one-hour lesson for Year Two. It's about parables. What parables can we think of?'

'The prodigal son… the good Samaritan… the lost sheep… the pearl of great price…'

'Those are all good. Should we do one in depth or several?'

'Just one; we should make sure they understand one well.'

'OK, but which would be best for a six-year-old? Is there one that particularly tells us what God is like?'

'How about the parable of the lost sheep? It's simple. The children will relate to losing something they care about and it can address other questions in the syllabus such as "What do Christians believe makes a person special?"'

'And we can make sheep, too! They'll enjoy that.'

'I agree it's pretty straightforward. But do children living in this city know what a shepherd does?'

'Well, maybe they could learn about being shepherds by acting out the story. They could make sheep and put them in a pen and count them. Maybe we could hide a sheep, then get them to discover that one's missing and find it.'

'I like the sound of that. But won't somebody get upset if their sheep goes missing? They are only six, after all.'

'Good point. How about if we make a sheep with our group and we hide that?'

'Will they still look for our sheep once they've found theirs?'

'Hey, that gives me an idea. We can look at another syllabus question: "How do Christians believe they should treat other people?" What if we start by acting out a story where someone is being mean to somebody else? We can get them to talk about the situation and how they would feel if it were them on the receiving end. When our sheep is lost, we can refer back to the story to encourage them to help us look for our sheep.'

'I think we are nearly there. We've got lots of different elements—craft, discussion, storytelling, active participation—and nothing will last too long. But we need a way to draw it together and to find out what they've learnt.'

'Could we find a different story that they will be familiar with, that has the same hidden meaning?'

'I think there's a Pingu episode where he runs away from home.'

'Perfect. I'll write this up and send it to the teacher and see what she thinks.'

Creating a session

The power of a session plan

This can be much more than a planning exercise, though. It's a means to secure positive partnership as well as inspiring strategies.

At the end of your conversation, invite different team members to prepare each element in the session, write up a draft outline and send it to your team for comments. You can be confident that the session will work because you've given your volunteers ownership and drawn on their creativity and experience. They know you are not asking them to do anything that's beyond them.

Arrange to meet the school's RE coordinator to talk about the lesson. Using the draft plan as a starting point, make sure that you are on the right track, shaping it in the light of the teacher's input. Discuss any preparation that might be helpful for the pupils in school and explore ways in which the topics can be picked up in class afterwards. This extension could be in RE or PSHE, but it could also happen across a range of learning areas.

RE is a compulsory subject, which is normally taught according to the locally agreed syllabus.[1] However, the pattern of teaching in many schools has been moving towards adopting creative learning strategies, which deliberately cross subject boundaries and emphasise creative skills such as listening, teamwork, dialogue and discussion.[2] These strategies have been expressed in different schools in quite different ways.[3]

RE most naturally relates to humanities subjects that require historical, geographical and social understanding. Here the overriding aim is to stimulate children's curiosity about the past and the present and their place in the world. The school should welcome efforts to place your session within the wider context of their pupils' learning. Discussing this in advance will give opportunity to the teachers to advise how your session can be connected to other aspects of recent or future learning.

At the end of the planning process, you will have sharpened the team's ideas so that they dovetail neatly with the school's needs, gained the teacher's trust by agreeing a plan for which you will be accountable, and received the school's approval for the session.

The plan then becomes a vital tool to ensure that everything is prepared in advance, keeps to time and gets covered on the day. You will be able to use it again and again, improving it every time. Also, if you are ever unwell or if you leave the team, others will be able to pick up the plan and use it with just as much confidence.

You'll find a version of our lesson plan for the parable of the lost sheep on page 115.

Thinking further

- Think about the way the session was developed above. Which steps did you think were important? What did you think of the lesson? What would you have done differently and why?
- Get hold of a copy of your local syllabus and look for touch-points where people of the Christian faith might bring a special contribution to learning. You may be able to download a copy from your local authority's website. If not, they will be able to supply a copy for a reasonable charge. Alternatively, make contact with a teacher at your local school and see if you can borrow a copy from the school's RE coordinator.

— Chapter 9 —

Creating a session (2)

The initial idea

In developing the session for the parable of the lost sheep, the original request to study a particular subject came from the school, and this is very common. The request may be quite general or may seek to answer specific syllabus questions. It's good to meet the needs of the school, but the initial idea for a lesson may also come from you.

You will know individuals in local churches with particular interests, talents and expertise, and you may be able to envision a great lesson that the teachers might not think to suggest. If there are talented artists and musicians available in the churches, you might be drawn to a session answering the question 'How do Christians express their beliefs through the arts?' But do remember two things.

- First of all, you are there to serve the school. Just because you think you've got a neat idea, it doesn't mean the school will agree. So don't invest too much time before you've spoken to the school, and be willing to take on board their ideas too.
- Secondly, schools are interested in a broad range of expressions of Christianity and other faiths, from which children can identify similarities and differences. That is why the ecumenical approach in education is so effective when partnering with schools, so you might wish to consider who else you could involve in your idea.

Putting it in context

In the story outlined in Chapter 8, our team leader, armed with a theme, turned to the local RE syllabus. She deduced the relevant questions and got her team together. Until you are confident in doing this, you might want to find out more by talking further to the school's RE coordinator. The RE coordinator will have a scheme of work which ensures that, during a Key Stage, all of the requirements of the locally agreed syllabus are met.

Spend time with the RE coordinator to find out why the scheme of work is the way it is, and to understand the progression in learning that it is designed to achieve. To make your lesson effective, you need to know what the children already know, the learning aims the teacher has set for your lesson, and how the teacher would like to connect it with other areas of learning and build on that knowledge later. If you fail to cover something essential, you may disappoint the school. This is another reason to ensure that you know the school's requirements before planning in detail.

The planning meeting

The next step in the story was to meet with the team to develop some ideas. As you gain experience, it may be tempting to plan the session yourself: you've got the experience, you know what works, and you can't face another meeting. Sometimes you will have to go it alone, but it's not ideal. You will have to sell your plan to your team rather than helping them buy into one of their own. Remember, your aim is to produce resilient lesson plans that are owned by the team, can be used by anybody and reflect the diversity of Christian beliefs and practices.

If you have a large pool of volunteers, you probably want to invite just a few of them to your meeting, but you might want to tell the others you are meeting and ask them to let you have any good ideas they might have. When inviting folk, remember that variety is good. If you are all of similar backgrounds, you may quickly come up with a plan that you all like, but you may never have considered some even better ideas.

In the story, our team leader was careful not to push her ideas but to draw out suggestions from the team. She is a facilitator: she sees her task as helping the team to come up with lots of ideas and to choose the best ones, moderating the discussion and keeping it focused on the aims of the lesson being planned.

The lesson plan

The lesson plan for the parable of the lost sheep lesson on page 115 follows a standard format that we use with these sessions. The format consists of:

- Curriculum questions
- Curriculum content
- Brief overview
- Links to wider curriculum
- Notes for teachers
- Schedule

Using a standard format makes it easy for everybody to look at a new lesson plan and know where to find the information they need, whatever their role.

Thinking further

- Choose a topic from your local syllabus and have a go at developing a lesson plan. Meet up with some people who might be interested in getting involved or enlist the help of another small group in church, such as a house group. Go back to basics and work out what the key points are and how to communicate them effectively.
- Send us a copy of the plan you produce and we'll be happy to discuss it with you. Maybe you are even ready to talk it through with your school's RE coordinator.
- Arrange to visit your local school and sit in on an RE lesson or two. How do you think the lesson you devised would help to support the teaching you've observed?

— Chapter 10 —

Nuts and bolts

School or church?

Settling on a venue is important in deciding what is possible for you to attempt. Most sessions benefit greatly from being held in a church space outside school. Many schools prefer to visit a church, and we like it that way. We can be more relaxed in setting up and clearing away. It's different from a normal lesson, the atmosphere in a place of worship sets a positive tone, and it breaks down negative stereotypes about church.

The 'lost sheep' session is usually run in a church setting, although it doesn't make special use of the church building itself. Other sessions depend much more on being in church. Baptism can be made more experiential when the children encounter a font or baptistry—even more so if you demonstrate what happens. Also, of course, if you want to talk about Christian symbols, a church will be a rich source of visual illustrations.

Sometimes the school will ask you to visit them. The distance to walk to the church may be too far, or, for the sake of sensitivity and balance, the school may prefer to host the session. If this is the case, it is important to be familiar with the space that the team will be working in, and to ensure that the room and any other equipment that you are relying on the school to provide are booked. Even when these arrangements have been made, being prepared to be flexible is important, as school is a very dynamic context to visit and things are liable to happen at the last moment.

If you are using a church, you will need to carry out a risk assessment and provide a copy to the school. A sample is available on pages 138–142.

Setting up

We generally allow an hour to set up before the children arrive, and we ask volunteers to arrive at least 30 minutes beforehand to prepare their bases, run through the lesson plan and pray together. Some teams look through the lesson plan over a cup of coffee. One team running sessions in the afternoon meets to set up at around 11.30am and discusses the lesson over lunch before praying and helping to walk the children from school. It's wonderful to spend time with Christians from other churches whom we would not otherwise meet.

Large and small groups

The sessions are usually introduced and led from the front, so there is always some work with the whole group of children. This gives an opportunity to introduce important ideas and reinforce learning for everyone. Sometimes we'll encourage the children to draw out key points and to express their opinions through open 'wondering' questions, such as 'I wonder… What would happen if…? What would it be like to…? What do you think it felt like…?' and so on. Generally, small groups are then used to explore the subject in more depth.

Small groups allow more children to contribute to discussions and provide opportunities for them to engage one-to-one with Christians about their beliefs. This is particularly beneficial to those lacking the confidence to ask or answer questions in a large group. However, it is often the pupils' best opportunity to interact with someone who has a Christian faith. They can ask their own questions about what Christians believe, why they pray and what their faith means to them, and can share something of their own beliefs with the adults as well. These are high-value conversations. Pupils rarely have this sort of learning opportunity. They will realise that these volunteers are not necessarily experts or church leaders. The conversations are not aimed so much at delivering 'correct answers' as communicating a sense of a person's faith.

In small or large groups, we aim to explore the subject in a number of different ways, keeping each activity short—no more than 20 minutes. The maximum duration of the session depends on the age group and the nature of the activity. Short activities mean that children stay focused.

Adopting different learning strategies

Pupils learn in different ways, so, apart from using different sorts of group work, most sessions will include a variety of different learning styles. One of the most powerful things you can do near the beginning of a session is to engage children by drawing on their experiences and their existing knowledge. Not only does this set the scene but also, for many, it says, 'They are interested in me' and 'I know something about this—I can contribute.'

DVDs can be a good way in to a straight telling of a Bible story.[1] Sometimes we also use clips from well-known films. From the leap of faith in *Indiana Jones and the Last Crusade* to episodes from *The Simpsons*, there are great illustrations to be drawn on. They visually grab the pupils' attention and help to present the topic in terms that they can access and in ways that are relevant for them. Do, however, make sure the location you use has an appropriate licence to show such clips.[2]

We also exploit the great tradition of oral storytelling. We may read a story straight from the Bible or we may tell it from a simplified children's version, such as *The Barnabas Children's Bible*.[3] We also use interactive stories in which children have an action to perform for some of the key words.[4]

Craft activities are kept simple so that everyone can create something worthwhile. They also need to be quick-drying and robust enough to make it back to the classroom or to home. The point is not to create a wonderful result but to provide a focus for reflection and discussion about what has just been taught.

There is no limit to the creative approaches you can adopt: puppetry, poetry, drama, music, whatever is imaginative and will work well is fine. However, we use very little written work—a sentence or two on a worksheet at most. This makes our lessons more accessible to those with special educational needs and more enjoyable all round. We are not, after all, trying to replicate a typical school lesson but to enrich the curriculum with something additional. We hope there will be windows of new understanding, positive memorable experiences of faith and church, and the possibility of spiritual discovery.

In particular, we aim to help the children demonstrate, through the work they produce and the questions they ask and answer, that they have both learned about religion and learned from religion. For example, if they have heard the story of the lost sheep, they have discussed what the story means; how Christians follow the example of Jesus by looking after others, even when they are annoying (learning about religion); how their own unkindness may cause others to feel, and how and why they might behave differently (learning from religion).

Who does what?

The small-group activities in our sessions are mostly suitable for an enthusiastic Christian volunteer to lead, regardless of the depth of their knowledge of Christianity. There are exceptions, particularly in some of the sessions for older children, but, by pairing experienced Christians with new volunteers, we provide opportunities for our leaders as well as the children to develop spiritually.

The session leader will often lead the whole-group work from the front, although this can be a shared role. However, the session leaders don't plan to run a small-group activity. This allows them to keep time and troubleshoot. They can move between the groups and adjust the time allocated in the plan if necessary. They can identify any points not covered or any interesting questions that need to be picked up and dealt with later in the session.

Review

After the lesson, we have a review session lasting between five and ten minutes. The team members report on what worked well and there are often suggestions for improving the session. It is also an opportunity to share humorous incidents and moments when we've seen significant spiritual learning. Indeed, it is often we who are learning. If anything has gone wrong, we can take action to correct it straight away.

The bigger picture

We hope you've caught a vision of how sessions can work, but there is still another layer of conversation to be explored with your RE coordinator in order to understand the bigger picture.

Looking at the local syllabus and their scheme of work together, you will be able to identify the best subject areas to which a team could contribute. It's tempting to think of Harvest, Christmas and Easter sessions as easy wins—and we do lots of them—but these topics are relatively straightforward for schools to cover. You may be able to add more value elsewhere, in areas of learning that staff are less comfortable teaching. Schools may be unfamiliar with them, lack confidence to present them or need an authentic answer to questions from a Christian perspective. However, stick to topics that you can present with confidence. If you want to do something seasonal, try Advent, Epiphany, Lent, Ascension or Pentecost, which are less well known.

By understanding how the syllabus is implemented, you can ensure that you don't repeat the same material for the same year group later on. You can layer further teaching on to earlier foundations and plan a learning path for each incoming class. We let that learning path build towards a fantastic final 'Difficult questions' session at the end of Year 6. In this session, the children get to ask a panel of Christians any questions they like about Christianity, and the panel gets to answer frankly but with sensitivity. Nothing is out of bounds: heaven, hell, death, sin, Satan, omniscience, suffering, big bang, evolution, creation, homosexuality, divorce or Christian beliefs about other faiths. Here is just a selection of questions from a recent session.

- God is meant to be the nice one, so why are people getting killed?
- Why is there war… and murder?
- Can God always see us?
- If there is a God, why doesn't he make everyone do good and worship him?
- What's heaven like?
- Will my kitten go to heaven?
- What are purity rings for?
- What was Jesus' full name?
- Do you pray to God or Jesus?
- Is the blood of Jesus still flowing?
- What does God actually do?
- How was God created?

These questions may sound daunting but you will be overwhelmed by the impact you can have on the spiritual development of the children. It is usual for serious, well-thought-out questions to start as a trickle and keep coming in waves until there is a sea of raised hands when the time is gone.

We'll leave the last word for the pupils.

The best bit was when we got to quiz the Christians at the end…

It's amazing how many things we don't know the answer to…

> ## **Thinking further**
> - List the creative strategies readily available, that you or others use already.
> - Select from these the ones most appropriate for work with schools.
> - How could you apply these strategies to the parable of the lost sheep, to achieve the learning aims from your local syllabus?

*

— Chapter 11 —

Spots, journalists and the arts

The parable of the lost sheep is just one of over 50 lesson plans we can now offer to schools. Every school is different—curriculum content can be delivered in different orders and in different ways—and the 'standard' sessions we have developed may not always add value as they stand. They might repeat material already covered or introduce topics that won't be picked up in class. There may also be something else that could be included, which would really help the teachers.

Having experienced our sessions, teachers sometimes gain the confidence to deliver more of the topics themselves. Serving the school and tailoring input around the teacher's needs is vital to building a stronger relationship. When we agree a programme of sessions with a school for the year ahead, we consider their whole RE programme and decide where our 'authentic Christian voice' can have the most impact on learning. It's an opportunity to be creative, to explore new subjects and deeper ideas, and to work towards a higher quality of input to RE at every stage of children's development.

Below are the outlines of three more lesson plans, employing different approaches for different Key Stages.

A lesson for children in Reception

'Spots began to appear on the earth'

Most churches will have someone who's good at sharing stories. Maybe they are leading your junior church or just reading to their grandchildren. They may not be confident about explaining what the story means—but they don't need to be. With younger children in particular, learning to listen to stories, recall what they've heard and express what they've understood are the skills that schools want them to develop. There is great value in working with the talent you've got and letting God fill in the gaps. We find that, as volunteers grow in confidence with their storytelling skills, they use their creativity to adapt ideas that work in church for use in a school context.

When one of our team members learned about the methodology of Godly Play,[1] she thought the reflective storytelling might work in school. Each session needs to be special to add something over and above a normal school lesson, to help young children remember and think about the story and its meaning. We thought the creation story would work well, and it does. This is what a delegate at one of our recent 'RE Matters' training days said:

I was very sceptical. The lack of eye contact goes against everything I'd learned about storytelling. But I was quickly drawn right into the story. The simple props encouraged you to use your imagination. I'll definitely have a go.

The teachers liked the way the children engaged with this story, and the artwork they produced afterwards clearly demonstrated that they had thought about it. A school asked if we could do something similar for Noah, so one of our volunteers wrote a Noah story for us. Now, equipped with an ark full of animals, some pieces of felt, a play parachute and a toy dove, we present the story of Noah in the following way to children in Reception classes.

We have up to 15 children gathered in a semicircle around the storyteller, who rolls out the felt shape representing the world—God's great gift. Then she lays out spots on the felt; first small ones, then larger ones. She says nothing about what the spots are, only that they started to appear on the earth and got bigger and bigger. When the earth is covered with spots, she says that God was sorry he had created the world and wanted to wash it clean, so he told Noah to build a boat and save the animals. At this point, the ark is brought out and the animals are presented for the children to identify and make the appropriate noises. When the story reaches the point where the ark has come to rest, the storyteller unfolds the parachute representing the rainbow, and tells the children about God's promise.

Next, we spend a few minutes asking open wondering questions about the story and allowing time for all the children to respond if they wish. Questions might include:

- I wonder what the spots could be…
- I wonder what it was like in the ark…
- I wonder which bit of the story you liked best…
- I wonder what the story is really telling us…

Responses we have had include:

Are the spots all the bad things people do, or maybe global warming?

It was nice of God to want to wash the world clean.

That's like the baptism of the world, that is.

Then we play some parachute games, finishing off in a 'mushroom' which becomes the ark, thinking about what it would have been like to be on board, and we act out sending out the dove. Finally everyone comes out of the ark and we recall God's promise and the sign of the rainbow.

A lesson plan for this session can be found on page 112.

A lesson for children at Key Stage One

The church visit revisited

Many churches already open their doors to school visits so that pupils can learn about their buildings. If yours doesn't, it's a great way to start working with schools. The locally agreed RE syllabus will almost certainly contain a requirement for pupils to learn about what happens in a Christian place of worship and the symbols that are used there. The best way to learn about what's in a church is to visit one. The best way to find out about what happens there is to talk to the people who worship there.

If your church meets in a school hall, leisure centre or home, you'll probably have to work with other churches on this one. But even the fact that you don't need a special building is, in itself, something important for children to learn about—and something that might not even be considered unless your voice is heard.

But how do you move beyond just offering a simple guided tour? How can you use the visit as an opportunity to develop a relationship? How do you help the children get the most out of it?

We turn the pupils into investigative journalists. We give each child a clipboard, pencil and worksheet with pictures of objects to find in the church, and send them on a quest to find out 'What happens in a place like this?' Depending on how relaxed you are, you can let them loose or you can wander around in supervised groups.

When they've found an object, they tick the box. To encourage the children to engage with the subject, they can also collect stickers with coloured pictures if they can ask our volunteers a good question about the things they see.

Back together, we draw out of the children the activities that the objects suggest might happen in church, and ask the children to respond by drawing the thing they think is most important in the church. We close by saying that while those things are all important, Christians believe that God thinks we are the most important thing in the church—and that's why he sent Jesus.

The format is fun for the kids, but it's much more than that. Rather than spending most of the time being expected to listen quietly, they are fully engaged throughout, seeking the information they need.

Another approach has been to set up 'stations' around the church for them to visit in groups. At each place, there is a 'hands on' opportunity for them to discover something. Examples include:

- To explore the special services that take place—being shown a christening or dedication roll and the marriage registers, learning about the indelible ink used to fill them in with, and even opening the church safe.
- To find out about the history of the church through looking at photos, discovering how old it is from a foundation stone, talking to an older church member and then putting together a large timeline puzzle.
- To be offered the experience of going into the pulpit to read the large pulpit Bible, or walk through an empty baptistry, or sit around the Communion table with the chalice, plates and Communion glasses and find out what happens there.
- To work out from a set of clues some of the other things that happen in the church during the week.

Each church will have different areas that work well. Conversations between leaders and children, used wisely, can tease out and develop the children's understanding rather than simply imparting knowledge. The shared experience and the worksheet they take back to school provide a base for teachers to build on in class. We develop their learning in later years with other sessions, such as Christian signs and symbols.

Even in a traditional church visit, you might expect comments such as those listed below, which were overheard on recent visits.

Wow, they've got a swimming pool.

It's not like my church—my church is a proper church.

They must think Jesus is very important.

The cross with Jesus on made me sad.

This approach can also give children the confidence to ask what a prayer board is for: they may respond by wanting to write their own prayers to put on it, prayers for those who are unwell or unemployed in their families.

A lesson plan for this session can be found on page 122.

A lesson for children at Key Stage Two

Faith and the arts

Well-designed sessions deliver knowledge about Christianity but also provide opportunities to learn from people who have a Christian faith. Sessions provide the opportunity for children to ask Christians, 'What do Christians believe?', 'How do Christians express their belief in their lives?' and 'How can I express my beliefs?'

One session that does this is entitled 'Faith in action'. In this session, Christians who work in the local community explain what they do and why they do it. They may be volunteers at a food bank or community police officers.

Another session is entitled 'Faith and the arts'. This is a wonderful celebration of creativity and diversity, which illustrates the benefits of bringing children into a church. It is extraordinarily creative and exploits all the benefits of churches working together.

The session on faith and the arts was originally planned to be in a traditional Anglican church which was also used by the Greek Orthodox

Church. We wanted the session to look at different aspects of art—such as music, painting, poetry, stained-glass windows, colours and embroidery in clerical vestments, drama and so on—but we also wanted to give the children an experience which would be difficult for them to have in their usual school environment. Using the icons from the Greek Orthodox Church was an obvious opportunity. A lay leader from the Greek Orthodox community agreed to share her knowledge with us and the children. The real value was in having someone who had a wide variety of icons to share and an in-depth knowledge of how and why they are made and used in that church. It was also interesting for the children to learn how this form of art is very different from the work of the modern artist who also contributes to the session.

CELIA STORRY, VOLUNTEER AND FORMER REINSPIRED TEAM COORDINATOR

We start with the children all together and show them a sequence of images of creation, inviting different responses, such as awe, wonder, amusement, 'aaahh' and so on. The children are always keen to tell us about their favourite image and why they like it; to relate the world around them to their emotions. We explain that we are made as creative beings in the image of God who created the world and us, and that many Christians express their feelings and their experience of God through art in one form or another. Different forms of art are mentioned and a Christian artist will show and talk about some of their paintings and invite the children to ask questions.

We then break into groups to do three of the following 15-minute activities in rotation. We choose the activities to suit the church we are using and the interests and experience of the individual teams. Each activity provides an opportunity to understand how Christians express their beliefs through an art form. Some enable the children to respond creatively to faith themselves.

Stained-glass windows

We show the children stained-glass windows and explain their origin as a way of teaching before mass-produced books were available. We identify some of the symbols and stories in the windows. The children make their own stained-glass window with coloured tissue paper fixed behind a window-shaped silhouette.

I really enjoyed when REinspired came to our school. It was really fun when we made our stained-glass windows. That was my favourite thing we did. I learned a lot and it really made me think about how beautiful the world around us is. It was a very enjoyable experience.

SOPHIE, YEAR 5

Banners

In one church, we show the children a series of seasonal banners created by a member of the congregation. We discuss the symbols used. The children might design their own banner or create one as a collage from pre-cut paper shapes.

Poetry

This might take the form of a reflection on a psalm. Psalm 139 is particularly good, as it can easily be illustrated with pictures and objects that the children can handle. Alternatively, we might look at poems and the words of hymns. We also encourage children to express their own spirituality by writing a simple haiku or acrostic poem on a word about faith or creation—for example, 'believe', 'cross', 'beauty' or 'creation'.

Music

We describe how Christians have written music and poetry to express their experiences of creation and God. We explain how Christians use music in church services and at other times to help them think about God and express their love for God in worship. Children are still developing the language to express their emotions at this age, but we look for ways to help them express what they feel. We invite them to listen to several pieces of music—classical, choral and modern worship songs—and then discuss whether the words (if there are any) and music fit with their emotions and feelings. Pupils from Whiteknights Primary School have made the following comments.

I liked listening to different music and seeing how it made us feel.

I was surprised there was some really funky music that made me want to dance.

Icons

A member of the Greek Orthodox Church shows the icons to the children and discusses their origin, purpose, features and how they are 'written' as an act of worship. The children can draw their favourite icon. Alternatively, as an icon is created in layers, so the class can work on creating their own 'icon' like one of those they've seen, with each group in turn adding a layer—first the background, then the figure and finally the features.

I really enjoyed REinspired. It made me think that there are lots of amazing things in the world. All the activities were really fun. Also, the people were very kind. My favourite part was seeing all the wonderful pictures.

AMY, YEAR 5

When we come back together, we invite the children to share something of what they have learnt or created. Sometimes, if the team is confident, we may finish with a piece of performance art, such as drama, dance or a rap.

A lesson plan for this session can be found on page 125.

Opportunities for spiritual awakening

In the session on faith and the arts, children engage creatively with faith themselves, as well as learning about how Christians do so. Once you have engaged them by relating faith to their own experience, pupils may be open to discuss their ideas and yours about the real spiritual questions with which they are grappling. Whatever session you are involved in, be alert to acknowledge and give time to respond to this level of engagement when it is offered by a pupil.

Thinking further

- How would you be prepared to respond to children engaging with spiritual questions at a personal level?
- When faced with a difficult question, do you need an expert or just an honest answer?

*

— Chapter 12 —

Difficult issues and challenging choices

Child protection

It's important from the outset to establish good child protection practice. It is tempting just to involve new volunteers straight away but this is always to be avoided. Ensuring that the correct paperwork is in place and that a proper induction of the new volunteer has taken place are vital. These things must be done efficiently and expeditiously in order to protect children, school, volunteers and project staff.

We work closely with our partner churches to ensure that all checks are undertaken before a volunteer starts. Having a satisfactory certificate from the Criminal Records Bureau is a prerequisite to being involved. If you don't, you can't. We require satisfactory references to be taken up and contact referees where appropriate to ensure their veracity.

In addition, legislation required that all staff and volunteers working with children would have to be registered with the Independent Safeguarding Authority (ISA) by November 2010. This is currently under review and the 'vetting and barring scheme' is being remodelled. However, by law you should not knowingly involve someone who is 'barred from working with children' and if you dismiss a member of staff or a volunteer because they have harmed a child or vulnerable adult, or you would have dismissed them if they had not left, you must tell the ISA.

It can become a mammoth job to keep on top of child protection issues as the number of volunteers grows. For us, it is a cooperative team effort. We have a formal child protection policy. We have a trustee to oversee this area of our work and use our team coordinators to fill in the paperwork with the volunteers as they come on board. Our project director ensures that everyone is on track with the different processes. We are also registered for advice, updates and support with a leading Christian child protection agency.[1] Most church denominations also issue advice to their churches in the light of government guidance and have advisers available for member churches.

Having a strong understanding of what constitutes good practice with school and volunteers is also important to prevent problems from arising. We ask all volunteers to sign that they agree to work within our good practice guidelines. It's important to ensure that responsibility lies where it needs to lie. We don't lead any sessions without a teacher present; if a child needs to go to the toilet, it is school staff who accompany them, and so on. Running this aspect of the work efficiently communicates to all that you take the issue seriously in a professional way, which, from a school's point of view, is a necessity.[2]

However, it is also important that volunteers know what to do if abuse is suspected or disclosed to them by a child during or after a session.[3] This has not happened in the ten years we have been running, but we would always want to be supportive of any child who found themselves in this situation. Being informed to know how to act is the minimum that such a child should expect of us. Some general ongoing training is essential, and we aim to cover this during our regular team meetings.

Team coordinators

Our first school team had a succession of three voluntary coordinators in four years before we moved to employ someone to lead it. The first was a minister, but the second and third were

Christians involved in a local church. We were amazed to see how, with careful management, the team and the school could adjust to so many changes of personnel in such a short time. The problems were eased because appointments came from within the existing team, but they also reflected the relational model that we have developed. These were people who understood the role from the inside, already knew the volunteers and some of the teaching staff involved, and had worked alongside the previous team coordinator.

As more schools started to ask us to work with them, however, it became clear that we needed to employ staff. We had to increase capacity and we couldn't rely only on volunteers to carry out the coordinator's role in all the teams. Moreover, as the responsibility of leadership grew, we wanted to reflect the value of their work by paying them. This was especially important as some key volunteers needed to return to paid work after having taken time off work to be with their young families, so REinspired had to either employ them or lose their gifts and experience.

Two coordinators started working for us for just six hours a week (term-time only), but this time commitment made an enormous difference. We now could rely on staff to lead and to take on the vital role of encouraging others. We later added further coordinators until we had four in post, each covering two or three of our eleven schools.

We asked them to develop links with the teaching staff at each school, identify what they felt they needed and recruit a team of volunteers to help address those needs. The schools' priorities varied enormously but the coordinators worked to devise sessions around those priorities, whatever they were. The schools' needs are always central, and that flexibility continues to be a key feature of our practice.

Difficult issues and challenging choices

Gifts, vocation and leadership for the project

There is a timeliness in 'God's economy', which distributes resources to points of need for mission. It is humbling to recall how many gifted people have been available to lead at critical moments. It challenges us to trust God more and to remember the lessons we learned from the journey for the next time we encounter them.

REinspired began life as 'The Churches Together in Earley and East Reading Schools Work Project'. Always a mouthful, its great strength was that it 'did what it said on the tin'. There had been a concern to support our local secondary school by leading collective worship, which went back 25 years. In 1994, we joined in with a town-wide mission and discovered that schools were more confident to invite us in as a group of churches than if we were working individually. Our Churches Together council decided that this was a 'lesson learned', which we should pursue in the future.

Later, one of our churches, a local ecumenical project, was struggling to appoint a part-time minister. The Bishop of Reading approached local ministers to ask if there was a contribution that could be made to the wider mission of the church in our area, to make up the post to a full-time role. Immediately we asked if someone could help us develop the relationships between our churches and the local schools. It was an inspired initiative and for eight years we benefited from a gift of 25 per cent of Revd Simon Howard's time from the Oxford Diocese. It was this wonderful appointment that laid the foundations for much of what followed.

The acceleration in demand from primary schools coincided with the departure of Simon to a new parish, so we took the decision to appoint Pete Stone, one of the coordinators, to a half-time post as Primary Development Worker. Having a 'figurehead' made an enormous difference. The number of sessions mushroomed and we quickly recognised the need to have someone other than a trustee to take the lead in other elements of the project, developing work with secondary schools, strengthening the links with churches, building a sustainable funding base and undertaking training.

After twelve months of trying to decide whether we could take the next financial step, we advertised for a full-time Project Manager. We were looking for someone who brought skills in education, theology and people and project management, but were disappointed when we couldn't find the right person. What we did learn was that we needed to be brave enough not to appoint if we weren't sure that the candidates brought the right mix of skills and approach.

It felt like a setback but it also presented an opportunity to allow someone from within the project to develop their skills in a new role. Following an interview, Pete Stone became our Project Manager. Under his care, the project continued to thrive and there were deepening links with head teachers, one of our Local Education Authorities and the church network.

Jane Earl, our chair of trustees, reflects on the significance of this decision.

The appointment of a full-time Project Manager was, financially, an act of faith, but it gave us the chance to move through several gears as a project. Pete was able to set the pattern for the systems and material which form the bedrock of our practice today. He also gave us a 'face' for REinspired which helped build relationships with head teachers, senior staff in the local authority and other key players. The relationship with schools flourished and the opportunities in school grew significantly. Without his post, we would not have moved so far or so fast.

We knew when we made this appointment that Pete was already thinking about another vocation. In the spring of 2008, he was accepted as a candidate for ordination in the Anglican Church. We celebrated this exciting step but were acutely aware that his loss would leave a huge gap in the project.

Once again we recruited, this time facilitated with the generous support of a local trust. Now we were looking for a Project Director. In late 2008, we were delighted to appoint Paul Haynes to the post. He, too, had a sense of vocation. He came to us with a background in IT and project management, alongside extensive church-based work with young people. Together with his strong faith, he has brought much-needed expertise into a developing project and a new richness to the work we do. Paul recalls his decision to apply.

I didn't know what God wanted me to do but I'd said 'yes' to God's call to serve him first and let him bless me. I'd made a step of faith in turning down a business opportunity. Almost immediately I was given an advert for 'An evening with Bob Hartman', organised by REinspired. What REinspired was doing sounded too good to be true—a way to be able to explain to all the local children about what we believe as Christians rather than to the handful in our churches. Though lacking theological or teaching qualifications, I just had to apply for the job. If nothing else, I might learn how to do it where I lived—and that's still my hope, to see the REinspired model adopted throughout the country.

With each appointment, we knew that the course we were following had significant consequences. It meant that we had to embrace a whole range of employment policies and practices; it also meant we needed to build our financial base in order to support our staff.

Thinking further

- Which of the issues we faced do you need to address now and which can wait?

*

— Chapter 13 —

The creation and evolution of REinspired

There is a profound sense in which the story of REinspired has been a journey of faith. There has been tremendous inspiration through creative ideas. In following the ideas through, the resources of personnel or money have rarely been sufficient but they have always been forthcoming.

An unfolding vision

In the challenge of a mission, there was a 'spark of inspiration' which for a moment illuminated Christian minds across our denominations. We had discovered that something could be achieved through working together with our schools. We were all acutely aware of the national concern that churches needed to reengage with younger people across our communities, and, in looking to support spiritual development in schools, we knew we were walking on ground that Christians have walked before us through history. The task seemed immense, but a decision was taken to do something about it and not to sit back and look on apathetically as the church became less and less relevant to young people.

At the outset, each church pledged just £200 per annum to create a fund to support this new venture. It was a small commitment but one that each community could make. It is interesting to see just how much you can do with modest amounts that are well directed. As the project has grown, those contributions have risen fivefold and more.

However, we didn't decide to build the project as it now is from the outset. It has developed as our understanding has grown and as we've engaged with schools. We chose to have a go, and what followed has evolved as God has guided and provided. The provision of funding from the Oxford Diocese and subsequently by the Jerusalem Trust, the Baptist Union and, most recently, the St Laurence Lands Trust, has come at strategic moments and stands as a reminder that we are making this journey in faith.

Our funding strategy has developed into three roughly equal parts: church giving, trust funds and donations from individuals. Each group of partners in our constituency of support needs continual attention, but this is true especially of our individual partner base, as people move and new partners need to be recruited. However, it is this personal, concerned, committed, prayerful foundation of financial support that is especially powerful and heartwarming.

Getting it right for staff

When we took on staff, we recognised that we needed to treat them properly and reward them appropriately, despite our limited resources. Our staff team has always given far more than we pay them for, and for this we continue to be profoundly grateful. We try not to take their good will for granted and, at the outset, we worked hard to put a number of provisions in place.

- A clear description of what we wanted them to do.
- Regular team meetings to provide mutual support, a sharing of good practice and a space for celebrating successes in addition to more informal input.
- One-to-one sessions with the Project Director to identify what support is needed and to work though any problems.
- An annual formal review meeting with the Project Director to discuss their development aspirations and opportunities.

- A planned session with the trustees to look at the development plan for the project.
- An annual pay review each September.
- Contributions to a stakeholder pension scheme.
- Opportunities to develop skills through training events, such as the Children's Ministry Conference.

In the early days, we needed to document a range of policies, which we now have in place. These included:

- Job descriptions.
- Contracts of employment, covering issues such as annual leave, hours of employment and review of performance processes.
- A health and safety policy for staff, including best practices for people working from home to keep them safe.
- An equal opportunities policy.
- A policy covering intellectual property rights so that material generated from REinspired became the property of the company.
- Processes to ensure that we could pay employers tax and National Insurance contributions.

'And the consequence was...'

We started with a 'Reference Group' to advise and work alongside Simon Howard, but we moved quickly to registering as a charity with a group of trustees, and established the project as a company limited by guarantee when we started to employ our own staff. Being a charity with trustees can work well in the short term and avoids all the paperwork that goes with being a limited company. However, our advice was to build for the long term and that a substantial project would expose trustees to large liabilities, so the choice to go for a limited company was more attractive.

We set out as a group of people with an interest in churches becoming involved in education. However, at the point when we needed a formal identity, we found ourselves out of our depth. We used a legal firm specialising in charitable companies to set us up as a company, register us as a charity and then act as Company Secretary for the first year. Retrospectively, it seems to have been money well spent.

There was a lot of paperwork. However, we were blessed by the expertise of a church member who had experience of running a small company and subsequently acted as Company Secretary. In addition, an experienced treasurer joined our group of trustees and took on the responsibilities of PAYE and producing proper accounts. Her expertise as an accountant helped to liberate other trustees for (in our eyes) more 'exciting' tasks.

A new name

As a byproduct of having to fill in the forms, we decided that a shorter, more eloquent name was needed to replace 'The Churches Together In Earley and East Reading Schools Work Project'. Becoming 'REinspired' coincided with a relaunch of the project to profile our new charitable identity. It reflected the fact that we had been developing over a long time and, in some ways, had arrived. Yet it was also true that we were still only setting out on our journey.

*

— Chapter 14 —

It's a gift

In 2009 we were spending approximately £50,000 per annum. If we include the amount of time that is offered and gifts in kind from churches, such as free use of premises, administrative support, gifts of staff time, the provision of office space and so on, we estimate that the total value of the project amounts to at least £100,000 per annum.

In primary education, we believe that there is little money available for the support of RE. It remains a 'Cinderella' subject that is largely not funded. There are always competing pressures on school funds and, although schools value our work highly, they would not be able to pay all our costs for the sessions we provide (around £300 a session). We are delighted that some of our schools have been willing to become 'contributing partners' but we remain realistic about the financial support that can be found from the primary schools themselves.

The relationship we seek

Fundamentally, we choose to offer our services as a 'gift' to the schools. We do this because it expresses the generosity inherent in the gospel. It is also important for us to be in a supportive, not a commercial, relationship with the schools so that while we are responding to the school's needs in all we do, we approach the educational task from the churches' perspective.

If schools recognise the contribution we bring and prioritise it financially, then we are delighted. If a local education authority would likewise value what we are doing and contribute to our core costs, that would be fantastic. To date, the former has happened and the latter is still an aspiration.

When it comes to offering additional special events, such as the 'transitional event' for primary school leavers, we often agree with schools to split the costs 50–50. If we offer schools or churches training support, it is normally offered at a professional rate.

How is the funding possible?

Direct church support is the mainstay of our financial position. It is a bedrock of support that, if requested, can often respond to the project's needs by offering inflation increases as well as a step change of giving when a growth point is reached. However, the advice we received when we were setting up was that direct church giving would probably, in time, be surpassed by individual donations, which attract income from tax reclaimed under Gift Aid regulations. Of course, having the endorsement of each funding church makes it more likely that individual partners will also be forthcoming from that community.

In working with trusts, it is interesting to note that they are often willing to support innovative work rather than core funding. This is particularly true of national groups. Local trusts are more willing to recognise the contribution being made to the local community. Being distinctively 'educational' rather than 'religious' is often a strength. Applying to trusts, and presenting well-argued plans for new work that falls within their criteria, is part of a way forward. Once you have other sources, contributing trusts are more likely to provide matching funding, but they will also want to see people on the ground taking responsibility for raising funds. Planning ahead and ensuring that your funding doesn't all come up for renewal at the same time is also wise.

Unsung heroes

Behind every successful project, there are a number of people who are, of necessity, grafting away at a range of issues. School practitioners need to get on with the task in hand but they need others who are working hard to build the relationships that keep the project on the road.

Jane Earl, our chair of trustees, reflects on this:

What makes REinspired so special isn't just the people who stand up in front of classes or lead inspirational assemblies. We also rely on people who may never be visible to our schools: the people who produce the newsletter; the administration work that goes on behind the scenes; the professionals who donate their time and skills to giving us financial, personnel or health and safety advice. And then there are those who get pulled into our work by accident or by relationship with someone else who is already involved. It's amazing how many partners of volunteers find themselves cutting out 30 pairs of hands from pink paper for a primary schools session, or contribute by proofreading documents.

Our philosophy is that everyone who is interested in helping can do something to contribute, and so, when we talk to churches or other groups of interested people, we always stress the 'behind the scenes' help that we value so highly.

We're deeply appreciative of our 'unsung heroes'. The good news is that when you are drawing on a pool of twelve or even 20 congregations, the experience you need will probably be available there if you look carefully.

— Chapter 15 —

A bigger project and an exciting question

REinspired is not involved just with RE in primary schools. This book has been written because RE is one of the distinctive elements of our practice with schools. However, like so many churches across the country, we regularly support collective worship and are also engaged in secondary schools.

Bottom up or top down?

Much of our thinking about this area of the churches' mission was born out of work at the other end of the school spectrum, in the sixth form. The reflection we've undertaken at the top of the secondary school has affected our practice at the bottom. Why? Because it's taught us to innovate in the ways we engage with students and to recognise the innate spirituality of students.

Across the country, 85 per cent of schools fail to offer any input towards the general RE entitlement of their students. As ever, RE is not properly funded at this level and, though compulsory, the entitlement is small and not well defined. For many schools, addressing great spiritual issues or exploring the value of RE with 16 to 19-year-olds seems like a task that's too hard to achieve and a turn-off for their students. In the past, school inspectors have often been pleased if there has been any positive attempt at all being made in this area.

Too difficult?

The assumption, you might conclude, is that students are not spiritual and can't connect to religious ideas, but nothing would be further from the truth. As we tried to develop our practice, we were invited by the Jerusalem Trust to participate in a new initiative with a national brief, which became known as 'dare2engage'.[1] Early on, D2E undertook research into the attitudes of students. Among other things, it found that students in this age group are 'more spiritual than religious and less atheistic than you may have thought'.[2]

Young people often reject the church and formalised religion but they are very much engaged with spiritual issues. Many are 'positive agnostics', those who lean sympathetically towards faith in their uncertainty about belief in God. Find a strong subject and some creative ways to explore it, and students will respond positively.

One outcome has been a range of road-tested, innovative resources from D2E designed especially for 16–19 settings in sixth forms, colleges and colleges of further education.[3] Another has been some surprisingly strong student evaluations of both sixth-form RE days and collective worship from local students. When a cohort of 160 students evaluates an RE day and only two students are disappointed, with the vast majority rating the day as 'very good' or 'good', or when they award their morning collective worship a score of 7.5 out of 10, something is connecting spiritually.

After a Year 12 sixth-form conference entitled 'An Evil Day',[4] these were some of the student evaluations from the 75 per cent who rated the day as 'very good' or 'good'. It is interesting to see the almost uniform expectations of an RE day and to contrast those expectations with the wide-ranging learning and thinking about their own spirituality that the students realised.

We asked, 'What did you expect this day would be like? What did you think about? and What did you learn today?' They answered:

A bigger project and an exciting question

I didn't know what to expect but I definitely thought I would die of boredom…

Everything. I'm thinking more about life, morals and feel I want to learn more about current events and history. I learnt that I need to think for myself. My views are important. It was stimulating, interesting, amusing and different.

FELICITY

Didn't expect anything; thought it would be boring…

There are plenty of people willing to make a change and I should too… Would've liked the session to be longer.

ASHDEEP

Long, boring…

I learnt to open my mind to questions for which perhaps I did not have an answer.

PETER

Boring with lots of talking for hours…

It was really good. I learnt that there is a lot of evil and I am evil in some ways. It should have been longer.

KATRINA

No idea…

Evil! How people can make a huge difference.

ED

Long and time-wasting…

I thought about my personal beliefs and my attitude towards life. I learnt that there are more important things in life than most things that I worry about.

AAESHA

Boring; I didn't think it would interest me…

I learnt to understand and listen to other people's views. I also learnt to explore my own views.

ELLEN

Lat Blaylock, as an RE adviser, makes the following observations.

One thing I notice about the way REinspired works with 16 to 19-year-olds is that the tutors in the sixth form have really come to trust REinspired, and this has happened because they can see the integrity and the ability to capture interest in spiritual questions that comes with the package. This is rare: many sixth forms know they should do some RE; few are privileged to be able to work with an outfit like REinspired to do so. I run lots of 16–19 RE activities around the country: dare2engage has enabled new ways of open-minded working to flourish, and published some resources that mean any Christian willing to prepare carefully can be involved in this rather exciting age group's spiritual quest.

An exciting question

If this is the sort of spiritual response that students are making now, what sort of response might we expect them to make if, as churches, we have been able to work consistently with them throughout their school careers?

The trouble with so much of our 'church into schools work' has been that there is input at the primary stages, and in lower secondary school, but it tends to fade out before students are making some of their most important personal decisions at 17 and 18 years of age. All of the investment in lower years is left to battle with the other huge pressures that dominate teenagers' lives today. At such a critical phase, it is vital that support to their spiritual development is sustained. There needs to be input that equips them to think about the answers to the great questions of life and belief and offers them credible models of faith to consider.

Continuity and consistency

REinspired is currently developing just such a programme of consistent input through the secondary years. We are at the stage where the children we worked with from Year 1 to Year 6, through primary school, are now coming into secondary school. It's exciting to find that, at the beginning of their secondary careers, we are one of the few elements in their new school that offer continuity with their primary experience. We're recognised and known.

We're experimenting with conference models in Year 9 RE, which, as in the sixth-form and primary models we use, break away from inherited patterns of learning and provide for a range of dynamic approaches to engage the subject.

It's different from primary school. The curriculum still offers spaces for 'people of faith' to speak, but the audience is increasingly discerning and challenging. There are still many resources in the churches, in terms of people who can contribute to schools wonderfully in specific areas. However, the curriculum here is much more specialist and defined, and the opportunities to include ordinary church members are fewer.

However, from thinking about 'What the Christian faith has to say about sexual ethics' through to questions about 'What makes a just war', there is much that currently engages the students. Indeed, there is a lot of encouragement in the fact that the number of pupils taking a formal course in RE at school, both at GCSE and AS level, makes RE among the fastest growing subjects at present.

— Chapter 16 —

Mission that will change your church

The great danger of getting stuck into schools work is that you can end up 'doing something to a school' rather than trying to work with a school, its teachers and students. We hope that your work will make a big impact, but not just on the students and school that you work with. We believe that a mark of 'good mission' is that we and our churches are also changed in the process. That, after all, is the way of Jesus, who became like us in order to do his Father's will.

If one mark of a healthy church is that it is focused outwards and engaged with the community around it,[1] then to engage with a local school is a brilliant way for an 'unhealthy' church to begin to recover its vigour. Our foundation document[2] states that 'our goal is… for local churches to become fully engaged in supporting local schools in the religious education and spiritual development of their pupils'.

Engagement with a school is not a shortcut to filling your church with young people; it is about enabling a generation to understand the Christian faith, to recognise its living power, to assess for themselves its truth and to draw down for themselves those things that are of value to them as they seek meaning in life.

It's a long-term strategy, which offers increasing opportunity. It doesn't need to grow to a large scale but could simply be part of what one church offers to its local school. However you see it, we hope you will discover it as a good place from which to begin.

* * *

On a visit with a schools inspector to the REinspired project, we were discussing the quality of the resource that was being delivered. The schools inspector remarked that this was a resource that could and should be promoted all over the country. This is a safe project for the children, for teachers, for schools, for the local authority, for the churches, but not a quick-fix project for anyone. Its intent is to have lasting value and longevity in the lives of all those who experience the project.

GILL CRIPPEN, REGIONAL MINISTER FOR MISSION STRATEGY
WITH THE SOUTHERN COUNTIES BAPTIST ASSOCIATION

If you think you've started to 'get it' and you're ready to 'do something with it', please look at our website for further details about the training and support available to help you get the work underway: www.reinspired.org.uk.

*

Epilogue

In Luke 10:38–42 we listen in to Jesus' conversation with two sisters. It reminds us of the privilege of learning about God, as well as the barriers that often prevent such spiritual discovery, and reveals Jesus' priority to open up such learning to others. One sister tries to communicate to the other that she wants her in the kitchen to help, while the other is listening as Jesus teaches. We often hear this story explained as Jesus' commentary on Martha's service and Mary's devotion. However, there is more going on than that.

Mary is sitting in the equivalent of a first-century Jewish classroom.[1] There are no chairs or desks but she sits with others at her rabbi's, or teacher's, feet. She is assuming the posture of a disciple or learner. Every rabbi had disciples and gathered them around him so that he could teach them. Mary adopted that position so that, one day, she too might perhaps teach others about God.

However, in that house, as in every other Jewish home at the time, the women would have sat separately from the men. It would have been quite unheard-of for a woman to sit among the men, learning about faith in God, yet Mary was doing just that.

Luke tells us that, unable to sort out the situation in any other way, Martha intervened: 'Finally, she went to Jesus and said, "Lord, doesn't it bother you that my sister has left me to do all the work by myself? Tell her to come and help me!"' (v. 40).

Jesus recognised that Martha was not concerned so much with dishes or food as with Mary's flagrant breaking of social conventions, with all the offence that it might produce. She finds it embarrassing, as Jesus seems to flag up: 'The Lord answered, "Martha, Martha! You are worried and upset about so many things, but only one thing is necessary. Mary has chosen what is best, and it will not be taken away from her"' (vv. 41–42).

Epilogue

The knowledge of God that Christians possess is no longer valued by society as it once was. Nonetheless, we are privileged to have received this gift of faith, so we need to ask God to lead us into fresh approaches, to ensure that the Christian faith is once again widely understood and appreciated. There are, of course, barriers to this activity in our increasingly sceptical and pluralist society, barriers that are not quickly overcome. Building trusting relationships with the staff of a local school and positively engaging with the needs and opportunities of the educational framework takes time. But, just as we might sometimes long to have sat at Jesus' feet in the rich place of spiritual learning and discovery that Mary enjoyed, so we, like Jesus, need to discover how we can develop creative spaces for today's young students, in which rich learning and spiritual growth can take place.

Appendices

— Appendix One —

Lesson plans

Spots began to appear on the earth (Reception)

Curriculum questions

- Area of exploration: Noah and the rainbow

Curriculum content

- Links to other learning themes: homes, the natural world, water

Brief overview

- Children will listen to the story of Noah.
- Children will play parachute games which reinforce elements of the story and provide opportunities for children to recall the story.

Links to wider curriculum

At the Foundation stage, schools are more likely to identify learning themes than discrete subject terms. The locally agreed syllabus used in the schools we work with identifies water, weather, the natural world and homes as learning themes to which the story of Noah and the rainbow might helpfully be related.

Appendix One: Lesson plans

Notes for teachers

- The lesson will last roughly 35 minutes and will be led by an ecumenical team of leaders and members of local churches.
- We are expecting 15 children.
- Please could each child wear a name badge.
- Please let us know about any special needs we need to consider.

Schedule

Introduction (2 minutes) (Storyteller)

The children enter and sit in a semicircle around the storyteller. The children are welcomed and told that we are not here to change their beliefs or faith, but to help them understand what Christians believe.

The storyteller then introduces him- or herself and his or her helpers and says:

'I am the storyteller—will you play the story of Noah with me? If you have any questions or want to tell me anything, please wait until the end of the story. Before we start, we have to make sure we are still on the inside and still on the outside. Are we ready? Then I'll begin.'

Story (15 minutes) (Storyteller)

The story of Noah is told using a script in a reflective storytelling style. The storyteller may read the story, or a helper may read the story while the storyteller plays it out with the toy animals and so on. The story can be sourced from a children's retelling of the Bible story or a modern Bible version such as the Contemporary English Version (CEV). The story can be found in Genesis 7:1—9:17.

NB: In the storytelling, no mention is made of wickedness or sin, which are represented by the spots appearing on the earth.

Children will be asked to wonder what the spots might be. For much of the story, eye contact with the children is avoided. This is deliberate and encourages children to focus on the story rather than the storyteller. Children rarely become disruptive; however, if this happens, a helper will move to sit with a child or take them away from the circle.

Parachute games (15 minutes) (Group leader)

- Game 1 involves becoming familiar with using the parachute and working together. Can the children make waves? Can they roll a ball around the chute? Can they lift the chute together?
- Game 2 involves shaking lots of foam spots off the parachute.
- Game 3 involves a coordinated effort to make a toy dove 'fly' as high as possible.
- Game 4 involves making a 'mushroom' in which children sit under the parachute. This forms an 'ark', in which we discuss what it would be like in Noah's ark. If there is a hole in the centre of the parachute, we pretend to send out the dove to look for dry land.

Resources needed

- Wooden Noah's ark set with pairs of animals.
- Script for Noah story.
- Large green felt square representing the land.
- Same-sized blue felt square, cut into strips of different widths, representing streams, rivers and so on.
- Black felt spots of different sizes representing 'sin'.
- Play parachute (ideally with hole in the centre).
- Foam spots (for parachute games).
- Soft toy dove (for parachute games).

Appendix One: Lesson plans

✻ ✻ ✻

The parable of the lost sheep (Years 1 and 2)

If you've used your team to pull together a plan, it will be different from ours. You will have volunteers with different skills, different experience and different passions. Maybe you don't have the equipment to show the Pingu clip. That's fine—just tell another story or find another way to tell the lost sheep parable. Maybe you want to cut out the story and spend longer on the craft. Maybe you prefer to choose a different parable altogether. After all, the school wanted a lesson on parables, and it was our decision to use this one.

Curriculum questions

- What did Jesus teach people about God?
- What stories did Jesus tell and why did he tell them?
- How do Christians believe they should treat other people?
- What do Christians believe about how people should live with others?
- What do Christians believe makes a person special?

Curriculum content

- Jesus taught and showed by example how God wanted people to live.
- The parable of the lost sheep describes Jesus' care for others and shows what God is like. Everyone is important to God.
- Jesus called God 'Father'.

- Christians understand that they are all members of God's family and he is their loving father. They should care for one another like brothers and sisters.

Brief overview

- Children will listen to the story of the lost sheep.
- There will be a craft activity in which they create their own flock.
- They will act the role of a good shepherd.
- We will learn that if we aspire to be like God, we need to aspire to be like the good shepherd.
- We will use a DVD clip, 'Pingu runs away', which has a similar underlying message.

NB: You should ensure that you have the appropriate permissions or licence to show DVD clips. If you have a Church Video Licence from Christian Copyright Licensing International, the Pingu film is by one of the producers covered by the scheme.

Links to wider curriculum

This subject was selected by the school and is clearly rooted in RE. Links to other areas of learning naturally relate to PSHE. At this stage in the curriculum, pupils should be learning about developing good relationships and respecting the differences between people. The following are natural touch-points, which can be drawn out as you work through the session.

- Family and friends should care for each other.
- It is important to listen to other people, and play and work cooperatively.

- It is important to identify and respect the differences and similarities between people.
- There are different types of teasing and bullying, and bullying is wrong. How do we get help to deal with bullying?

Notes for teachers

- The lesson will last roughly one hour and will be led by an ecumenical team of leaders and members of local churches.
- We are expecting 60 children.
- Please could each child wear a name badge.
- Please divide the children into six groups of ten beforehand.
- Please let us know about any special needs we need to consider.
- It would be brilliant if children could come dressed as 'biblical' shepherds—for example, with tea towels on heads, and dressing-gowns.

Schedule

Introduction (10 minutes) (Session leader)

The children sit together in one large group. The children are welcomed and told that we are not here to change their beliefs or faith, but to help them understand what Christians believe.

The session leader introduces the day's session. Today's session is about parables—stories with a meaning; stories that can teach us about life, what is right and wrong, what God is like and how he wants us to treat others.

Two helpers act out a story in which one person hides the other's toy as a prank (if it's a sheep, so much the better). Children are invited to play 'hot and cold' to help find the hidden toy. Make sure it's obvious that somebody is upset, that it was unkind to hide the toy, and that it is good to say sorry and make up afterwards.

Children are sent to their groups of ten to talk about the story they've just seen.

Activity one (5 minutes) (Group leader)

Have a group discussion about the story. Can the children tell you what happened? Use questions such as these to see if the children understood the underlying message:

- How did each person feel?
- Did their feelings change?
- What was right and what was wrong?
- How easy is it to say sorry and to forgive?
- How would the children feel if something similar happened to them?
- If children have done something like this to another person themselves, did they realise how upset the other person might be? How might they behave differently in future?

Tell children about the golden rule: treat others how you would like to be treated, like brothers and sisters.

Shepherds need sheep (8 minutes) (Session leader)

The children come back together into one group. The session leader asks them questions to draw out the meaning of the story, to make sure everybody understands it. The children are told that the golden rule was one of many things Jesus taught us about how to live. Often he taught using stories. Jesus was a great storyteller. Say, 'This toy sheep [if used] reminds me of a story Jesus told about a shepherd and some sheep. Jesus was often referred to as the good shepherd. God is like the good shepherd. Christians try to be more like God: he is their role model—their hero, if you like.' Tell the children how great they look as shepherds but that shepherds need sheep to look after.

The children are asked to go to their groups and to talk about what it means to be a shepherd, and then make their sheep.

Activity two (10 minutes) (Group leader)

Each child has a piece of card cut out like a sheep. The children write their name on the back of the card, draw a face on the front, and stick cotton wool on the sheep.

What do shepherds do? (5 minutes) (Session leader)

The children come back together. Tell them what a shepherd does and how important it is to make sure all the sheep are counted in at the end of the day. Send them to their groups to count their sheep.

Activity three (2 minutes) (Group leader)

Mark out a 'sheep pen' on the table or floor using masking tape. Leave an opening. Get the children to count the sheep into the pen, making sure they are really certain about how many sheep are there.

Story (10 minutes) (Session leader)

The children come back together. Tell them that after the sheep are safely counted, the shepherds have their supper and tell stories before going to sleep. Say, 'I'm going to tell you a story Jesus told about the good shepherd.' Read the story from a children's retelling of the Bible[1] and say, 'Now I think it's time for bed.' Before they settle down to sleep, ask the 'shepherds' to think of all the things they are going to do tomorrow—taking the flock to a new field that has fresh grass, and so on. Ask the children to close their eyes, relax and pretend to sleep. Morning comes, and the birds are chirping. What would a good shepherd do first, before his or her cornflakes? That's right—check the sheep.

Send children to their groups to check their sheep. While the children were 'asleep', each group leader has removed his or her own sheep from the pen and hidden it.

Activity four (5 minutes) (Group leader)

Children return to their bases to count their sheep. Encourage the children to look for the lost sheep. Remind them of the golden rule: even though it's not their sheep that's been lost, it's kind of them to look for the missing sheep.

Conclusion (10 minutes) (Session leader)

The children come back together and are congratulated on finding their lost sheep. They are also asked, 'If the same sheep got out again, would you go after him a second time? How many times would you go after him? Would you get bored and give up? What do you think the good shepherd would do?'

Say, 'We have just learnt the story of the good shepherd. It's just one of the stories that Jesus told to help people understand what God is like and how he wants us to behave towards each other. In this case, it means that he wants us to care for one another like a shepherd does for the sheep. The shepherd loves them and cares for them, even when they wander off and get lost. Even if people keep on wandering off and it gets annoying, Christians believe we should forgive them and stick with them.'

Modern stories have lessons in them, too. Say that you are going to see a clip from *Pingu*, and explain its relevance. Pingu gets cross and runs away, but he soon gets into trouble and is lost and frightened.

Play *Pingu's Big Video*, story 11, 'Pingu runs away'.[2]

Say, 'Did you hear the message in the story? Who do you think was like the lost sheep? Who was like the shepherd? Even when we do wrong things, people still love us and come and help us. You

Ask the children some questions to see what they've learnt:

- Why did Jesus tell the story?
- What do Christians think God is like?
- If God is like the good shepherd, who are the sheep?
- How do Christians think we should treat others?
- What do Christians think makes a person special?

Thank the children for joining in and say goodbye. Remind them to take their sheep with them.

Resources needed

- Six volunteers and one coordinator
- A children's retelling of the Bible story
- Toy sheep
- DVD: *Pingu's Big Video*
- DVD player or PC, projector, screen and loud speakers
- Six sets of felt-tip pens and glue sticks
- 60 sheep shapes cut out of white card
- Bag of cotton wool (one ball per sheep)
- Wobbly eyes for sheep
- Blu-Tack
- Feedback forms, pens and clipboards for teachers

The story of REinspired

* * *

A church visit (Key Stage One)

Curriculum questions

- How and why do Christians use symbols in everyday life, places of worship, and celebrations?
- How do Christians use their places of worship?

Curriculum content

- Christian symbols such as a cross and crucifix, hot cross buns and Easter eggs, cribs, Christingle, dove, water.
- Symbolic features of churches such as lights and candles, festivals and celebrations, clerical dress, Salvation Army uniform and so on.
- Going to church, including how prayer and music are used, reading the Bible, Sunday as a special day, as well as coming into church at other times and for other activities.

Brief overview

- Children will hear that we can learn a lot about people by the things they do and the things they have around them.
- Children will wander around the church, looking for objects that are shown on the worksheet.
- Children are asked to decide what they think is the most important thing they've seen in the church.

Appendix One: Lesson plans

Links to wider curriculum

Visiting a church is an ideal way for teachers to help children progress in history, geography and social understanding by finding out about:

- Key human and physical features of their own locality and how these features have changed over time.
- Lives of significant people and events from past and present.

Visiting several churches (different denominations, urban and suburban, old and modern) provides richer opportunities, whether students visit all the churches together or in small groups and report back. Comparing and contrasting helps to develop thinking skills, but can also add depth to history and geography projects.

Notes for teachers

- The lesson will last roughly 45 minutes and will be led by an ecumenical team of leaders and members of local churches.
- We are expecting 60 children.
- Please could each child wear a name badge.
- Please let us know about any special needs we need to consider.

Schedule

Introduction (10 minutes) (Session leader)

The children sit together in one large group. The children are welcomed and told that we are not here to change their beliefs or faith, but to help them understand what Christians believe.

Introduce the day's session: 'I wonder what your special place is—somewhere where you feel safe and secure? *(Invite answers.)* For many of you, that might be your bedroom, where you might have lots of special things. I expect I could tell a lot about you from the special things you have in your bedroom. I wonder what I'd find in your bedroom. *(Invite answers.)* Well, today we're in a church, and I wonder whether you can find out what goes on here by looking around at what's inside.'

Hand out worksheets and explain how to tick off objects when they are found or how to collect stickers.

Wander and wonder (25 minutes) (Group leaders)

Children wander freely around the church. Volunteers are placed strategically to point children towards objects, answer questions, and also ask questions to help children piece together a picture of the things that go on.

Conclusion (10 minutes) (Session leader)

The children come back together. As individuals finish and return to the front, they are asked about what they have seen and whether the evidence points towards any activities that might take place in church. They are also asked to draw the object they think is most important on the back of their worksheet. The session leader draws out answers about the activities that take place in the church.

Finish with the observation that Christians believe that, important though all these things are, to God, people are even more important.

Resources needed

- 60 clipboards and pencils
- 60 worksheets with pictures of objects that can be found in the church
- 60 sets of stickers with colour pictures of the objects on the worksheet (optional)

Appendix One: Lesson plans

✻ ✻ ✻

Faith and the arts (Key Stage Two)

Curriculum questions

- How do Christians express their beliefs through the arts?

Curriculum content

- Examples of Christian beliefs expressed in the arts, such as paintings, sculptures, architecture, drama, literature, music and the use of the Bible as the basis for songs, films and so on.

Brief overview

- The children will all start together in one group, then divide into smaller groups to work around three bases, experiencing a variety of mediums such as pictures, crafts, reading and listening. They will take worksheets back to the classroom with them.

Links to the wider curriculum

There are obvious links from this session to the wider curriculum in art and music. Poetry provides opportunities to connect to literacy, the chance to write a poem and to reflect on a Christian reading of psalms and other poems. Stained-glass windows provoke questions about history, technology and communications. Recognising the emotions we feel when we hear music is relevant to PSHE.

Notes for teachers

- The lesson will last roughly 70 minutes and will be led by an ecumenical team of leaders and members of local churches.
- We are expecting 60 children.
- Please could each child wear a name badge.
- Please divide the children into six groups of ten beforehand.
- Please let us know about any special needs we need to consider.

Schedule

Introduction (10 minutes) (Session leader)

The children are welcomed and told that we are not here to change their beliefs or faith, but to help them understand what Christians believe.

Show a PowerPoint presentation of images of creation. Invite the children to share their favourite images. Say that the very first people wondered why and how the world was created when they looked at everything around them—animals, plants, stars, mountains, rivers, seasons, day and night, people and so on. People of all faiths feel that there is a mighty force that we call God, who has created everything in the world. A sense of wonder and awe has been in people's minds since the beginning of time. As people became more sophisticated, they expressed this sense of wonder and awe through drawings and paintings (found first on cave walls), through dance, models, music, song, poetry, stories, stained-glass windows and photography... all these are forms of art.

Activity 1 (10 minutes) (Guest interview)

Interview somebody who is a Christian and an artist about why they paint, how they started painting and so on. If a Christian artist is not available, show some pictures of Christian art.

Appendix One: Lesson plans

Question-and-answer session from the children (Session leader)

Split into groups and visit the following three bases in turn:

- **Base 1 (15 minutes):** Stained-glass windows. The children will be shown pictures of stained-glass windows and told the stories and meanings behind them.
  - ❖ *Craft activity:* children make their own stained-glass window with black card and coloured tissue paper.

- **Base 2 (15 minutes):** Music. The children will listen to different types of music and say which they like most. What does the music make them think about? Think of some of the lovely things in the world. Christians use very different sorts of music to worship God—from classical pieces, perhaps played on an organ, to simple plainsong, and traditional hymns led by choirs to more modern songs and contemporary music (perhaps play some examples). Sometimes movement and dance are used too.

- **Base 3 (15 minutes):** Poetry. Leaders share a poem, a psalm, a hymn or a haiku expressing wonder and awe about things in the world.
  - ❖ *Children respond:* Which do they like best, and why? What words did they like? What did the words express? They then either draw a picture of one of the poems or make an acrostic using a significant word, such as 'SPRING'. If there is time, they might even write their own poem.

Conclusion (5 minutes) (Session leader)

You can conclude the session by summarising the different forms of artistic expression that the children have seen. Remind them that God and Jesus are so important to Christians that Christians express their faith in all sorts of ways in their lives—in church and throughout the week. If they are musicians, they express their faith through music; if they are artists, through painting, drawing and sculpture; if they are poets, through poetry, and so on.

Explain that most Christians aren't great artists or musicians, but they often enjoy and find it helpful to look at pictures or listen to music to help them think about God and to inspire their worship.

Suggest that perhaps, when the children feel particularly happy, sad, excited or frustrated, they might find it helpful to let the feelings out through art. Also, when they next see a painting, they might think about what the artist is really trying to tell us.

If you have the appropriate skills within your team, you might finish with a drama, rap or dance. Say that you will leave the children with one more art form. Suggest that when they get back to class, they might like to talk about what the author, writer or choreographer was trying to say.

Resources needed

- Six volunteers and one coordinator
- 60 black cards with window shape cut out
- Coloured tissue paper for stained-glass windows
- Pictures of stained-glass windows (unless you are in a church with stained-glass windows)
- CD player and CD of appropriate music
- Collection of poems, psalms and hymn lyrics
- 60 worksheets
- A laptop, projector and PA system to show a slideshow of pictures of the world we live in
- Slideshow of Christian art pictures (if an artist is unable to come to show and talk about their work)

Appendix One: Lesson plans

***

Death, funerals and the Christian response (Years 5 and 6)

Curriculum questions

- How and why do Christians mark a person's death?
- What do Christians believe about life after death?
- How do Christian beliefs about life after death influence the way Christian people live their lives?

Curriculum content

- What happens at funerals?
- How does a funeral illustrate Christian beliefs about life after death?
- What is the impact of Jesus' death and resurrection on Christian beliefs?

Brief overview

- What happens at a funeral?
- Different styles within the Christian traditions of church.
- What Christians believe happens after death: a hope of heaven.
- The impact of Jesus' death and resurrection.
- What belief about Jesus' death and resurrection means for Christians.

Three workshops to consider

- A personal response to a death: exploring the nature of grief, the progression from grief to thanksgiving, and the Christian perspective on life, death and the life to come. Exploring the idea that we are only here for a 'season'—'on loan', as it were—and life on earth is only part of our journey.
- What do people do to mark a person's death? Also consider how we want to be remembered: what will our legacy be? How does this influence the way we live now?
- Journeying on: read *Waterbugs and Dragonflies*,[3] a story to illustrate what happens next. Reflect on themes of new life, a hope of heaven, that death is a natural progression and nothing to be frightened of.

Links to wider curriculum

- Many schools cover World War I in Year 6, and some schools that we work with visit the battlefields in France. This ties in with the memorial base, in which we show and discuss war memorials and military cemeteries.
- The grief base is relevant to PSHE, covering topics that many teachers are not confident in tackling. The model of change discussed can be widely applied to coping with other forms of loss and change.
- The story of the waterbug is based on the biological lifecycle of the dragonfly, so it provides touch-points with science.

Appendix One: Lesson plans

Notes for teachers

- The length of the visit is 1 hour and 30 minutes.
- We are expecting around 60 children.
- Please divide the children into six groups of ten beforehand.
- Please could the children wear numbered name badges.
- The visit will be led by an ecumenical group of church members and church leaders.
- There will be experienced adult helpers for each small group.
- Are there any children with special needs, for whom we should make provision?
- Are there any children who have suffered bereavement recently, for whom we should make provision?

Schedule

The children are welcomed and told that we are not here to change their beliefs or faith, but to help them understand what Christians believe.

Introduction (13 minutes) (Leader or guest priest)

Has anyone been to a funeral? What do the children think the point of a funeral is? Explain what happens in the practical sense in your own tradition and what a funeral means to Christians. Explain that other Christian traditions may conduct a funeral differently.

Explore the idea of letting go, mourning, celebrating the person's life, and thanking God for 'loaning' them to us.

Explain that Christians believe that Jesus' death and resurrection are proof of God's power over nature and creation, life and death and the universe.

Explain that Christians believe that those who have died are now in God's care again: belief in Jesus' death and resurrection leads to a Christian's hope of heaven.

Divide the children into their groups of ten and explain that each group will visit three bases, covering the following topics. Each base is replicated once, to avoid having too many children at each base. (Ensure that you have enough group leaders to cover all six bases.)

- 1 and 4: A person's personal response to death
- 2 and 5: What people might do to mark a person's death
- 3 and 6: A Christian's hope of heaven (*Waterbugs and Dragonflies*)

Bases 1 / 4 (18 minutes)

The aim of this base is to explore grief—what it is and how it makes us feel—using the idea of the 'seven stages of grief'.[4] On a large piece of paper, mind-map how the children think they would feel, or have felt, in response to the death of someone they know. Children will be familiar with the idea of listing ideas and organising them as a mind map (which they may know as a spider diagram). The aim is not to get a correct model of the grieving process but to help children share their experiences, thoughts and fears.

You will find that, collectively, they come up with many of the feelings you would expect, and the feelings can generally be grouped under the different stages of the model. You may find that some of the feelings the children suggest are unusual, but explore why they suggested them and ask if others agree. Finally, you can discuss a possible order in which the seven stages are likely to occur, but explain that the stages are not intended to be a rigid framework. Alternatively, you can show the seven stages of grief towards the end of your discussion.

Reflect with the pupils on whether they think grieving and its associated feelings are normal. Explain that grieving is a natural response and nothing to be afraid of. It is part of the healing process; it needs to be worked through and is a journey in itself. We can only feel grief if we have loved. Explore how grief is about us and how we feel. It is a 'self-indulgent' but necessary part of healing.

Appendix One: Lesson plans

Explain how a Christian belief in Jesus' resurrection helps people through the journey of grief. Christians believe that God is with them in their suffering. Take the 'seven stages of grief' picture that has a cross at every stage of grief, and place it next to the previous one. Grieving helps us through the process when we lose someone or something that is precious to us. On the floor, lay the first heart with the words 'Christians believe that God is with them in their suffering' written on it. If possible, share a personal experience of grief.

God knows what grief is like. Christians believe that death is not the end. On the floor, lay the second heart with the words 'Christians believe that Jesus' resurrection proves that death is not the end' written on it. Say that Christians believe that the dead person has returned to God. This gives a Christian comfort and hope. They can then begin to think of thanking God for the person's life. They can remember the good things and happy times, and thank God for sharing that person with them. Lay the first statement card on the floor: 'It is better to have loved and lost…'. Ask, 'I wonder what you feel about this…?' and use the question to open up a discussion.

Lay the second statement card on the floor: 'I wonder what this teaches us about how we should treat people while we have them in our lives…?' Explore the nature of love and what it means to the children. Talk about a Christian belief of what love is. Refer to 1 Corinthians 13:4–8 ('Love is patient and kind…'). Thank the children for sharing their thoughts and ideas and ask if they have any questions.

Invite the children to fill in the first part of the worksheet on page 144.

Bases 2 / 5 (18 minutes)

Mind-map some things that people might do to mark a person's death, and look at resources (see below or source local and personal items and books).

Show the children things that mark a person's death, such as an obituary in a newspaper; pictures of gravestones, memorials and epitaphs; flowers (explore the language of flowers and colours); poems; music; living legacies, such as Great Ormond Street Children's Hospital or Peter Pan. Ask how the children would want to be remembered. Lay on the floor the thought bubble with the words 'What would I like to be remembered for?' Ask the children to write down what they would want to be remembered for.

Ask how their response reflects the way they are living now. Explain that Christians believe that they have part of their life's journey on earth and that they have been given a task to do while they are here. Talk about the 'golden rule'.[5] Would our legacy or epitaph reflect the golden rule?

Lay the second thought bubble on the floor, with the wording 'Have I loved God?' Explain that loving God is one of the things that motivates Christians to live the way that they do. Christians believe that they must try to love other people as much as they love themselves. Explain what this means personally to you as a Christian.

Mind-map what a Christian does to show that they love other people and that they want to love and worship God. Explore the idea of a Christian being a good disciple of Jesus.

Fill in the second part of the worksheet on page 144.

Bases 3 / 6 (18 minutes)

Use the book *Waterbugs and Dragonflies* to tell the story. Ask the children what they think of the story. Which bit do they like best? What do they think is the most important part? The story illustrates how death is just change—journeying on.

Ask the children to make a dragonfly picture. (See the resources list on pages 136–137 and the craft activity instructions on page 145.)

Fill in the final part of the worksheet on page 144.

Overview

Return to the large group and overview the session. Ask the children what they have learnt today. Underline that grief is a natural response to loss. Christians believe that death is not the end because of what happened to Jesus, and that God is with them in their suffering and helps them through it. They also believe that God is waiting to welcome them into heaven when the time comes. Believing this affects the way Christians live their lives.

Play a clip from the DVD *The Lord of the Rings: The Return of the King*, scene selection 38. Run the clip forward a little to 2:02.19 and run to 2:03.35 on the counter. The scene is 'A far green country', where Gandalf talks to Pippin about the next life.

NB: this is a 12 certificate film, so you will need to check with the school about their policy before showing it to Year 6 students. Approximate times have been given to narrow the scene right down to focus on the conversation between Pippin and Gandalf, but you may have to practise this on your own system before the session to get it spot on.

Conclusion

Finish by explaining that none of us can know what heaven is really like. Like the dragonflies in the story, those who have died cannot come back to tell others about it. We may all be curious but, for Christians, their faith and their relationship with God give them confidence that there is a life after death and that, when the time comes, God is waiting to welcome them home.

Pause to reflect before saying a final farewell.

Resources needed

NB: Make sure that you have checked with the school whether there are any children who are grieving at the moment or have been bereaved in the past year.

For Bases 1 / 4

- Worksheet (see page 144), pens and clipboard (one per child).
- Seven cards with one of the seven stages of grief printed on each, and seven small cardboard or paper crosses.
- Large pieces of paper and felt-tipped pens.
- Two hearts cut out of card, one with the words 'Christians believe that God is with them in their suffering' and one with the words 'Christians believe that Jesus' resurrection proves that death is not the end'.
- Two statement cards, one with the words 'It is better to have loved and lost…' and the other with the words 'I wonder what this teaches us about how we should treat people while we have them in our lives…'

For Bases 2 / 5

- Items that mark a person's death, such as an obituary in a newspaper; pictures of gravestones, memorials and epitaphs; fresh flowers; a selection of your own poems; CDs; hymn books; pictures that show a legacy such as Great Ormond Street Children's Hospital or Peter Pan.
- Two thought bubble cards, one with the wording 'What would I like to be remembered for?' and one with the wording 'Have I loved God?'
- Paper and pens.

For Bases 3 / 6

- The story *Waterbugs and Dragonflies* by Doris Stickney.
- One sheet of A4 card or paper per child, with the wording on page 146 written or pre-printed at top and bottom.
- Dragonfly body and wings pre-cut from the template on page 147.
- Wobbly eyes (optional).

- Small sticky pads.
- Colouring materials and glue sticks.

For large group

- A DVD of *The Lord of the Rings: The Return of the King* (Scene selection 38).
- A DVD player, projector, screen and PA system. (The dialogue is softly spoken, so the volume may need to be turned up).

— Appendix Two —

Sample risk assessment

Given below, as an example, is a risk assessment we completed recently in advance of a local school visit. You'll need to devise your own form so that you can identify issues you may meet and decide how you will manage them with the school, should they occur.

Risk assessment for Earley St Peter's Church

For [enter name of school] _____

Hazard or activity	Risk associated with the hazards	Risk	Controls already in place and action required by school
Walking through the front gate and along the graveyard path to the church entrance	Slipping, tripping, falling	Low	Children will be supervised at all times by the school staff.
Walking from the south porch around the front of the church on the graveyard path to the main church entrance	Slipping, tripping, falling	Low	As above.

Appendix Two: Sample risk assessment

Hazard or activity	Risk associated with the hazards	Risk	Controls already in place and action required by school
Walking up a step to enter the vestry or south porch of the church, or walking up or down any steps within the church—for example, to the pulpit, to the lectern, from the chancel to the Lady Chapel, in the chancel	Slipping, tripping, falling	Low	School staff and children should take care climbing steps to avoid tripping and falling. Children will be supervised by a REinspired team member or school staff at all times.
Electrical equipment (data projector)	Tripping over electrical cables trailing from power source to equipment; electric shock due to tampering with equipment	Low	Children are seated at a safe distance from all equipment. If children are moving around the building, a member of the REinspired team stands by the cables to ensure that children keep a safe distance. Loose cables are covered. Regular PAT Tests are carried out.

Hazard or activity	Risk associated with the hazards	Risk	Controls already in place and action required by school
Fire	Inhalation, skin burns, panic, loss of control	Low	In case of fire: • Appropriate equipment is in place within the church building. • REinspired team leader will direct staff and children towards nearest exit; emergency exits are clearly labelled. • School staff should ensure that they and children in their care leave the building by the nearest exit. • Assemble in car park at the front of the church hall by the church yard. • School staff should ensure that a roll call is taken of their charges.
Using scissors and other craft items	Cuts to fingers; injury inflicted by other children	Medium	Scissors are kept in a sealed box when not in use. Craft activities designed are appropriate to the age group involved. There will be continuous supervision by REinspired volunteers and school staff. There are regular checks of equipment to ensure that all items are safe to use.

Appendix Two: Sample risk assessment

Hazard or activity	Risk associated with the hazards	Risk	Controls already in place and action required by school
Climbing on chairs or pews	Falling	Low	Younger children are seated on the floor. Children must be adequately supervised and instructed not to climb on chairs.
Entering the building and walking from base to base, up and down steps	Tripping, falling, bumping	Low	Children are clearly instructed as to which direction to take and how to get there (walk, not run, and so on). Carpets and other floor coverings are regularly maintained.
Visiting the toilet in the church hall	Contact with inappropriate adults. Walking along the graveyard paths and across the car park, cars moving, slipping, tripping, falling and so on.	Low	Any child needing to use the toilet must be accompanied by a member of school staff (or their representative) and not a member of the REinspired team or any other adult. (See page 88 for information about the ISA registration procedures and CRB clearance undertaken by all REinspired staff.)
Children leaving the church without supervision	Lost child; accident in the car park or road outside church; contact with other adults	Low	All external doors are kept closed during the visit. Children are supervised at all times. Members of the school staff are responsible for counting in and counting out children.

Hazard or activity	Risk associated with the hazards	Risk	Controls already in place and action required by school
Occasional use of candles under adult supervision	Children burning themselves or each other; starting a fire; hot wax dripping on to skin	Low	Matches are held by an adult at all times. Wax catchers are placed around individual candles which pupils hold. All candle lighting, holding and looking is supervised at all times by a member of the REinspired team or school staff.

Signature _____ (REinspired coordinator)

Date _____

— Appendix Three —

Templates

The following templates can also be downloaded free of charge from the website www.barnabasinchurches.org.uk/7716.

Death, funerals and the Christian response worksheet

This sheet is for you to write down anything you want from this session today. It may be something that surprised you, it may be something new that you learned today, or it might be a question that you still have.

Grief

How do you want to be remembered?

Waterbugs and dragonflies

Name_____ Class_____

Dragonfly craft activity

This activity follows the reading of the story by Doris Stickney and a discussion about its meaning.

You will need:
- One sheet of A4 card or paper per child, with the wording from page 146 written or printed on it
- Dragonfly bodies and wings (see page 147 for template)
- Painting and colouring materials
- *Optional:* two wobbly eyes per dragonfly (self-adhesive if possible)

Preparation

- Cut out one body and one set of wings for each child from bright, ideally iridescent or metallic paper (see page 147). Alternatively, pre-cut kits can be ordered from Infinite (www.inf.co.uk) in bulk.
- Write or print the wording below on to the sheets of A4 card or paper to form a background for the dragonfly (see page 146 for layout). Preprinted sheets can be downloaded free of charge from www.barnabasinchurches.org.uk/7716 or www.reinspired.org.uk.
  ❖ Waterbugs and dragonflies.
  ❖ 'I guess I'll have to wait until they become dragonflies too. Then they'll understand what happened to me and where I went.' DORIS STICKNEY

Activity

Ask the children to draw a reed shape on their card or paper. Glue the dragonfly body to the reed shape. Glue the dragonfly wings to the body, leaving the ends of the wings to flap. Fix the wobbly eyes to the dragonfly's head. Decorate the background to represent water, sky, vegetation and so on.

Waterbugs and dragonflies

'I guess I'll have to wait until they become dragonflies too. Then they'll understand what happened to me and where I went.'

DORIS STICKNEY

Dragonfly body and wings

*

Notes

Introduction

1. *Waterbugs and Dragonflies*, Doris Stickney (Pilgrim Press, 1982; Continuum, 2002).
2. www.reinspired.org.uk.

Chapter 2

1. www.freshexpressions.org.uk.
2. Religious Education in English Schools: Non-statutory guidance 2010 (QCDA), p. 4.
3. Religious Education in English Schools: Non-statutory guidance 2010, p. 12.
4. Non-statutory National Framework for Religious Education (QCDA, 2004).
5. Section 78 (1) of the 2002 Education Act.
6. Non-statutory National Framework for Religious Education (QCDA, 2004), pp. 8, 14–15.
7. Religious Education in English Schools: Non-statutory guidance 2010, p. 7.
8. Lat Blaylock is editor of *RE Today* magazine and has written many resources for RE. He also advises teachers, schools, SACREs, dioceses and local authorities. He runs day conferences for gifted and talented pupils and for 16 to 19-year-olds.
9. Religious Education in English Schools: Non-statutory guidance 2010, p. 4.
10. Religious Education in English Schools: Non-statutory guidance 2010, p. 38.
11. Religious Education in English Schools: Non-statutory guidance 2010, p. 32.

Chapter 3

1. Acts 17:16.
2. Acts 17:22.
3. Religious Education in English Schools: Non-statutory guidance 2010, pp. 8 and 7.
4. Acts 17:18b.
5. Non-statutory National Framework for Religious Education, 2004, p. 7.
6. Religious Education in English Schools: Non-statutory guidance 2010, p. 10.
7. Acts 17:23.
8. Religious Education in English Schools: Non-statutory guidance 2010, p. 7.

Chapter 4

1. To see an example of Razwan's work alongside Christians, visit www.teachers.tv/videos/ks4-re-faith-and-form-exploring-the-physical-aspects-of-religion.

Chapter 7

1. More information is available at www.transforminglives.org.uk.
2. Romans 8:31.
3. You can find out more about Godly Play at www.godlyplay.org.uk.
4. Bob Hartman has written a wide range of resources for telling Christian stories. We most frequently use *The Lion Storyteller Bible* (Lion Hudson, 1995).

Chapter 8

1. Religious Education in English Schools: Non-statutory guidance 2010.
2. The seminal report *All Our Futures* (DfES 1999: 2) argued that, to meet the challenges of the 21st century, there is a

need to nurture a creative curriculum that develops young people's capacities for original ideas and action.
3. *Lifting the Lid on the Creative Curriculum*, Tim Burgess (National College for School Leadership, 2007).

Chapter 10

1. For example, *Friends and Heroes*, 2009 (Friends and Heroes Productions) or *Miracle Maker* DVD, 2000.
2. Any public showing of films or TV programmes, even small clips, will violate copyright law unless you have a licence to play them in public. Fortunately, films shown in schools as part of a lesson do not generally count as a public performance (Copyright, Designs, and Patents Act 1988, chapter III, subsections 32–36.) However, if you show the same clip to a school visiting your church, it would be regarded as a public performance and needs a licence. You could consider contacting the copyright holder of each film you want to show individually, but it is probably more practical to obtain a Church Video Licence from Christian Copyright Licensing International, which covers many film producers. The licence does not cover all film producers so you do still need to check whether the films you want to show are covered. Details of CCLI licensing can be found at www.ccli.co.uk/licences/churches_showing-films.cfm, and a list of producers covered by the scheme can be found at www.ccli.co.uk/pdfs/CVL-Producers-UK-Eire.pdf.
3. *The Barnabas Children's Bible*, Rhona Davies (Barnabas, 2007). Available also as *The Barnabas Schools' Bible*, Rhona Davies (Barnabas, 2007).
4. *Telling the Bible*, Bob Hartman (Monarch, 2006).

Chapter 11

1. Godly Play is a particular approach. You can find out more about it at www.godlyplay.org.uk.

Chapter 12

1. The Churches' Child Protection Advisory Service: www.ccpas.co.uk.
2. A copy of the popular version of our child protection policy and good practice guidelines can be found at www.reinspired.org.uk/cpp
3. See REinspired Child Protection Policy and Guidance: www.reinspired.org.uk/cpp.

Chapter 15

1. www.dare2engage.org.
2. 'Seventeen year olds: more spiritual than religious, less atheistic than you may have thought', written by Lat Blaylock, data analysis by Peter Williams, in *Resource* (Autumn 2005). Also available free of charge from the dare2engage website at www.dare2engage.org, posted 30 May 2007.
3. 'Spiritual Engagement' is a selection of RE days for 16–19s available from RE Today. 'Rage and Despair' is an RE day published in partnership with Bible Society. 'Breathe' is an art installation which works well in a number of settings with 16–19s. 'Festive' is an initiative working in FE and sixth-form colleges.
4. 'An Evil Day' is one of the RE days featured in 'Spiritual Engagement'.

Chapter 16

1. Robert Warren, *Healthy Churches' Handbook: A Process for Revitalising Your Church* (CHP, 2004).
2. Available at www.reinspired.org.uk.

Epilogue

1. *Luke for Everyone*, Tom Wright (SPCK, 2001).

Appendix One

1. For example, *The Barnabas Schools' Bible*, Rhona Davies, or *The Lion Storyteller Bible*, Bob Hartman.
2. *Pingu's Big Video* (BBC, 1998).
3. *Waterbugs and Dragonflies*, Doris Stickney.
4. For information on the seven stages of grief, see, for example, www.recover-from-grief.com/7-stages-of-grief.html and http://changingminds.org/disciplines/change_management/kubler_ross/kubler_ross.htm. The seven stages of grief are a modification of the Kübler-Ross model, commonly known as the five stages of grief, which was first introduced by Elisabeth Kübler-Ross in her book *On Death and Dying* (Macmillan, 1969).
5. Many ethics systems include statements about having a right to fair treatment and a responsibility to treat others fairly. This is commonly known as the 'golden rule'. For Christians, it is embodied in Jesus' teaching in Luke 6:27–36 on loving our enemies, and verse 31 in particular: 'Treat others just as you want to be treated.'

Also from BRF/Barnabas

The Barnabas Schools' Bible

Including Bible encyclopedia

Rhona Davies

Illustrated by Marcin Piwowarski

This new Children's Bible includes stories chosen to cover all the main events, retold with a continuous thread.

There are 365 stories, one for every day of the year, each accompanied by Bible quotations from a real Bible translation, giving readers a taste of the language and style of the original texts.

The stylish illustrations illuminate and inform, while the easily accessible encyclopedia at the end of the book helps to explain the context and background of the stories. All combine to make this a useful and readable Bible for older children.

ISBN 978 1 84101 564 4   £12.99
To order, you may use the order form on page 159. Alternatively, please visit www.brfonline.org.uk.

Also from BRF/Barnabas

Local Church, Local School

Practical and creative ways for churches to serve local primary schools

Margaret Withers

Local Church, Local School is intended for church leaders, lay leaders, children's work leaders, governors, PTAs, teaching staff, non-teaching staff and Christian parents seeking to support and serve their local primary schools.

The aim of the book is to encourage churches to see engagement with their local schools as part of their service in the community. This can be as much through presence and practical support as through teaching and leading worship, and has the added bonus of giving confidence to schools to see their local church as a teaching resource as well as being a community with much to offer.

The book provides practical ideas and well-founded information on all aspects of engagement, including theological considerations, identifying opportunities and skills, getting involved, and the creative use of respective buildings. Above all, it enables church members to understand how the spiritual needs of the school fit into the legal requirements of the RE programme and the big picture of the school day.

ISBN 978 1 84101 586 6   £8.99
To order, you may use the order form on page 159. Alternatively, please visit www.brfonline.org.uk.

Also from BRF/Barnabas

Story Assemblies for the School Year

36 assemblies with five-minute stories, teacher's notes and RE follow-up

Edward J. Carter

This book is full of memorable stories, designed to engage and delight pupils at primary level. The stories are essentially parables about God and the events in the Bible, creatively told to help children understand the big story of God's love for the world.

There are six themes in total, each with its own easy-to-make storytelling prop. The stories within each theme are divided into six weekly episodes, covering a wide range of contemporary values and topics. Together the stories cover the whole school year, with a key theme and a story in six parts for each half-term period.

As well as being ideal for collective worship, there are practical follow-up ideas to help children connect with the stories in the classroom.

The six themes cover God's creation; the message of the Old Testament prophets; stories about Christian values; the story of Holy Week and Easter; Jesus' resurrection and ascension; and the journeys of the apostle Paul.

ISBN 978 1 84101 699 3   £8.99
To order, you may use the order form on page 159. Alternatively, please visit www.brfonline.org.uk.

Also from BRF/Barnabas

Stories for Interactive Assemblies

15 story-based assemblies to get children talking

Nigel Bishop

Collective worship is an ideal time to combine biblical teaching with contemporary storytelling. The 15 easy-to-tell, contemporary stories in this book are all based in the world of the classroom but have their roots in the parables of Jesus. They are designed to stimulate children's thinking and get them talking in the assembly and afterwards in the classroom.

Each story is followed by questions designed to help the children interact with the issues raised, plus suggestions for practical activities, based on different learning styles. Each story also includes:

- A target theme to help direct the teacher towards the main teaching objective.
- A prayer or reflection to close the assembly if desired.
- Bible references for the original parables.
- Information to link the teaching to PSHE/Citizenship and the non-statutory national framework for RE or local SACRE guidelines.

ISBN 978 1 84101 465 4 £6.99
To order, you may use the order form on page 159. Alternatively, please visit www.brfonline.org.uk.

Also from BRF/Barnabas

Reflective Learning

Unpacking key Christian beliefs in RE and collective worship

Trevor Reader and Lilian Weatherley

Reflective Learning provides essential background information for key Christian beliefs and offers important tools to instil confidence in the teaching of RE. The material focuses on three key concepts related to the principal beliefs of the Christian faith:

- **Who God is (the Trinity):** Three units comprising the stories of creation, re-creation and baptism.
- **What God has done (Salvation):** Five units comprising the stories of Christmas and Epiphany, Lent, Holy Week, Easter and Pentecost.
- **The Church today (Reflective living):** Three units relating to the journey of life.

Each unit starts with an in-depth classroom-based exploration of the concept. The classroom material is supported by two comprehensive outlines for acts of collective worship.

Alongside the class work and assembly material, creative ideas are given for setting up a theme-based focus table for the classroom.

ISBN 978 1 84101 573 6   £8.99

To order, you may use the order form on page 159. Alternatively, please visit www.brfonline.org.uk.

ORDER FORM

REF	TITLE	PRICE	QTY	TOTAL
564 4	The Barnabas Schools' Bible	£12.99		
586 6	Local Church, Local School	£8.99		
699 3	Story Assemblies for the School Year	£8.99		
465 4	Stories for Interactive Assemblies	£6.99		
573 6	Reflective Learning	£8.99		

POSTAGE AND PACKING CHARGES

Order value	UK	Europe	Surface	Air Mail
£7.00 & under	£1.25	£3.00	£3.50	£5.50
£7.10–£30.00	£2.25	£5.50	£6.50	£10.00
Over £30.00	FREE	prices on request		

Postage and packing
Donation
TOTAL

Name _____ Account Number _____

Address _____

_____ Postcode _____

Telephone Number _____

Email _____

Payment by: ❑ Cheque ❑ Mastercard ❑ Visa ❑ Postal Order ❑ Maestro

Card no ☐☐☐☐ ☐☐☐☐ ☐☐☐☐ ☐☐☐☐ ☐☐☐

Valid from ☐☐☐☐ Expires ☐☐☐☐ Issue no. ☐☐☐

Security code* ☐☐☐ *Last 3 digits on the reverse of the card. ESSENTIAL IN ORDER TO PROCESS YOUR ORDER

Shaded boxes for Maestro use only

Signature _____ Date _____

All orders must be accompanied by the appropriate payment.

Please send your completed order form to:
BRF, 15 The Chambers, Vineyard, Abingdon OX14 3FE
Tel. 01865 319700 / Fax. 01865 319701 Email: enquiries@brf.org.uk

❑ Please send me further information about BRF publications.

Available from your local Christian bookshop.   BRF is a Registered Charity

About brf:

BRF is a registered charity and also a limited company, and has been in existence since 1922. Through all that we do—producing resources, providing training, working face-to-face with adults and children, and via the web—we work to resource individuals and church communities in their Christian discipleship through the Bible, prayer and worship.

Our Barnabas children's team works with primary schools and churches to help children under 11, and the adults who work with them, to explore Christianity creatively and to bring the Bible alive.

To find out more about BRF and its core activities and ministries, visit:

www.brf.org.uk
www.brfonline.org.uk
www.barnabasinschools.org.uk
www.barnabasinchurches.org.uk
www.messychurch.org.uk
www.foundations21.org.uk

If you have any questions about BRF and our work, please email us at

enquiries@brf.org.uk